ART OF

ACHIEVING SUCCESS

FOUR CLASSICS THAT HAVE CHANGED LIVES:

...THE MAGIC STORY
...AS A MAN THINKETH
...ACRES OF DIAMONDS
...THE RICHEST MAN IN BABYLON

COMPILED BY JOHN D. HAWKES

TABLE OF CONTENTS

FOREWORD

Life is a challenge and everyone would like to accomplish more, to have more and to do more with life's brief moments. The excuse that is universally rendered is that we would do more "if" we only had more time and capital. In reality the problem is not more time or money, but more **MOTIVATION!** With proper motivation, time will be better organized and utilized. Capital will come to those who show evidence that they can be a success.

The four classics can have a great influence for good in creating a positive philosophy and stirring the motivation needed to achieve. The compiler has added summary remarks on the four classics and then has organized a **SUCCESS FORMULA** that should lead you to a more successful life. The publishers are in hopes that the reader will not only read and study this book, but will learn to apply its principles, thereby acquiring the success personality and the art of achieving success.

THE MAGIC STORY

I was sitting alone in the cafe, and had just reached for the sugar preparatory to putting it into my coffee. Outside the weather was hideous. Snow and sleet came swirling down, and howled frightfully. Every time the outer door opened a draft of unwelcome air penetrated the uttermost corners of the room. Still, I was comfortable. The snow and sleet and wind conveyed nothing to me except an abstract thanksgiving that I was where it could not affect me. While I dreamed and sipped my coffee, the door opened and closed, and admitted-Sturtevant.

Sturtevant was an undeniable failure, but, withal, an artist of more than ordinary talent. He had however, fallen into the rut traveled by ne'er-do-wells, and was out at the elbows as well as insolvent.

As I raised my eyes to Sturtevant's I was conscious of mild surprise at the change of his appearance. Yet he was not dressed differently. He wore the same threadbare coat in which he always appeared, and the old brown hat was the same. And yet there was something new and strange in his appearance. As he swished his hat around to relieve it of the burden of snow deposited by the howling nor'wester, there was something new in the gesticulation. I could not remember when I had invited Sturtevant to dine with me, but involuntarily I beckoned to him. He nodded, and presently seated himself opposite to me. I ask him what he would have, and he, after scanning the bill of fare, carelessly, ordered from it leisurely, and invited me to join him in coffee for two. I watched him in stupid wonder, but, as I had invited the obligation, I was prepared to pay for it, although I knew I hadn't sufficient cash to settle the bill. Meanwhile I noted with increasing amazement the brightness of his usual lack-luster eyes, and the healthful, hopeful glow upon his cheek.

"Have you lost a rich uncle?" I asked.

"No," he replied calmly, "but I have found my mascot."

"Brindle bull or terrier?" I inquired.

"Currier," said Sturtevant, at length pausing with his coffee cup half way to his lips, "I see that I have surprised you. It is not strange for I am a surprise to myself. I am a new man, a different man-and the alteration has taken place in the last few hours. You have seen me come into this place 'broke' many a time, when you have turned away, so that I would think you did not see me. I knew why you did that. It was not because you did not want to pay for a dinner, but because you did not have the money to do it. Is that your check? Let me have it. Thank you. I haven't any money with me tonight, but I,-well, this is my treat."

He called the waiter to him, and, with an inimitable flourish, signed his name on the backs of the two checks, and waved him away. After that he was silent a moment while he looked into my eyes, smiling at the astonishment which I in vain strove to conceal.

"Do you know an artist who possesses more talent than I?" he asked, presently "No. Do you happen to know anything in the line of my profession that I could not accomplish, if I applied myself to it? No. You have been a reporter on the dailies for-how many?-seven or eight years. Do you remember when I ever had any credit until tonight? No. Was I refused just now? You have seen for yourself. Tomorrow my new career begins. Within a month I shall have a bank account. Why? Because I have discovered the secret of success.

"Yes," he continued, when I did not reply, "my fortune is made. I have been reading a strange story, and, since reading it, I feel that my fortune is assured. It will make your fortune too. All you have to do is to read it. You have no idea what it will do for you. Nothing is impossible after you know that story. It makes everything as plain as A, B, C. The very instant you grasp its true meaning, sucess is is certain. This morning I was a hopeless, aimless bit of garbage in the metropolitan ash can; tonight I wouldn't change places with a millionaire. That sounds foolish, but it is true. The millionaire has spent his enthusiasm; mine is all at hand."

"You amaze me," I said, wondering if he had been drinking absinthe. "Won't you tell me the story? I should like to hear it."

"Certainly. I mean to tell it to the whole world. It is really remarkable that it should have been written and should remain in print so long, with never a soul to appreciate it until now. This morning I was starving. I hadn't any credit, nor a place to get a meal. I was seriously meditating suicide. I had gone to three of the papers for which I had done work, and had been handed back all that I had submitted. I had to choose quickly between death by suicide and death slowly by starvation. **THEN I FOUND THE STORY AND READ IT.** You can hardly imagine the transformation. Why, my dear boy, everything is changed at once and there you are.

"But what is the story, Sturtevant?"

"Wait; let me finish. I took those same old drawings to other editors, and every one of them was accepted at once.

"Can the story do for others what it has done for you? For example, would it be of assistance to me?" I asked.

"Help you? Why not? Listen and I will tell you, although,really, you should read it. Still, I will tell it as best I can. It is like this: you see-"

The waiter interrupted us at that moment. He informed Sturtevant that he was wanted at the telephone, and with a word of apology, the artist left the table. Five minutes later I saw him rush out into the sleet and wind and disappear. Within the recollection of the frequenters of that cafe, Sturtevant had never before been called out by telephone. That, of itself, was substantial proof of a change in his circumstances.

One night, on the street, I encountered Avery, a former college chum, then a reporter on one of the evening papers. It was about a month after my memorable interview with Sturtevant, which, by that time, was almost forgotten.

"Hello, old chap," he said, "how's the world using you? Still on space?"

"Yes, I replied bitterly, "with prospects of being on the town shortly. But you look as if things were coming your way. Tell me all about it."

"Things have been coming my way, for a fact, and it is all remarkable, when all is said. You know Sturtevant, don't you? It's all due to him. I was plumb down on my luck-thinking of the morgue and all that-looking for you, in fact, with the idea that you would lend me enough to pay my room rent, when I met Sturtevant. He told me a story, and really, old man, it is the most remarkable story you ever heard; it made a new man of me. Within twenty four hours I was on my feet, and I've hardly known a care or a trouble since."

Avery's statement, uttered calmly, and with the air of one who had merely pronounced an axiom, recalled to my mind the conversation with Sturtevant in the cafe that stormy night, nearly a month before.

"It must be a remarkable story," I said, incredulously. "Sturtevant mentioned it to me once. I have not seen him since. Where is he now?"

"He has been making war sketches in Cuba, at two hundred a week; he's just returned. It is a fact that everybody who has heard that story has done well since. There are Cosgrove and Phillips-friends of mine-you don't know them. One's a real estate agent; the other a broker's clerk. Sturtevant told them the story, and they have experienced the same results that I have; and they are not the only ones, either."

"Do you know the story?" I asked. "Will you try its effect on me?"

"Certainly, with the greatest pleasure in the world. I would like to have it printed in big black type, and posted on the elevated stations throughout New York. It certainly would do a lot of good and it's as simple as A, B, C; like living on a farm. Excuse me a minute, will you? I see Danforth over there. Back in a minute, old Chap."

He nodded and smiled-and was gone. I saw him join the man he had designated as Danforth. My attention was distracted for a moment, and, when I looked again, BOTH HAD DISAPPEARED.

If the truth be told, I was hungry. My pocket at that moment contained exactly five cents, just enough to pay for my fare uptown, but insufficient also to stand the expense of filling my stomach. There was a "night owl" wagon in the neighborhood, where I had frequently "stood up" the purveyor of midnight dainties, and to him I applied. He was leaving the station as I was on the point of entering it, and I accosted him.

"I'm broke again," I said, with extreme cordiality. You'll have to trust me once more. Some ham and eggs, I think will do for the present."

He coughed, hesitated a moment, and then re-entered the wagon with me.

"Mr. Currier is good for anything he orders," he said to the man in charge, "one of my old customers. His is Mr. Bryan, Mr. Currier. He will take care of you, and stand for you, just the same as I would. The fact is, I have sold out. I've just turned over the outfit to Bryan. By the way, isn't Sturtevant a friend of yours?"

I nodded I couldn't have spoken if I had tried.

"Well," continued the ex-'night-owl' man, "he came here one night, about a month ago, and told me the most wonderful story I ever heard. I've just bought a place on Eighth Avenue, where I am going to run a regular restaurant-near Twenty-third Street. Come and see me."

He was out of the wagon, and the sliding door had been banged shut before I could stop him; so I ate my ham and eggs in silence, and resolved that I would hear that story before I slept. If it had made so many fortunes, surely it should be capable of making mine.

The certainty that the wonderful story-(I began to regard it as magic)-was in the air possessed me. As I started to walk homeward, fingering the solitary nickel in my pocket and contemplating the certainty of riding down town in the morning, I experienced the sensation of something stealthily pursuing me, as if Fate were treading along behind me, yet never overtaking, and I was conscious that I was possessed with or by the story. When I reached Union Square, I examined my address book for the home of Sturtevant. It was not recorded there. Then I remembered the cafe in University Place, and, although the hour was late, it occurred to me that he might be there.

He was! In a far corner of the room, surrounded by a group of acquaintances I saw him. He discovered me at the same instant, and motioned to me to join them at the table. There was no chance for the story however. There were half a dozen around the table, and I was the farthest removed from Sturtevant. But I kept my eyes upon him, and bided my time, determined that, when he rose to depart, I would go with him. A silence, suggestive of respectful awe, had fallen upon the party when I took my seat. Every one seemed to be thinking, and the attention of all was fixed upon Sturtevant. The cause was apparent. He had been telling the story. I had entered the cafe just too late to hear it. On my right, when I took my seat, was a doctor; on my left a lawyer. Facing me on the other side was a novelist with whom I had some acquaintance. The others were artists and newspaper men.

"It's too bad, Mr. Currier," remarked the doctor, "you should have come a little sooner. Sturtevant had been telling us a story; it is quite wonderful, really. I say, Sturtevant, won't you tell that story again, for the benefit of Mr. Currier?"

"Why, yes. I believe that Curier has, somehow, failed to hear the magic story, although, as a matter of fact, I think he was the first one to whom I mentioned it at all. It was here, in this cafe, too, at this very table. Do you

remember what a wild night that was, Currie? Wasn't I
called to the telephone, or something like that? To be sure!
I remember, now, interrupted just at the point when I was
beginning the story. After that, I told it to three or four
fellows, and it 'braced them up,' as it had me. It seems
incredible that a mere story can have such a tonic effect
upon the success of so many persons who are engaged in
such widely different occupations, but that is what it has
done. It is a kind of never-failing remedy, like a cough
mixture that is warranted to cure everything from a cold
in the head to galloping consumption. There was Parsons,
for example. He is a broker, you know, and had been on the
wrong side of the market for a month. He had utterly lost
his grip, and was on the verge of failure. I happened to
meet him at the time he was feeling the bluest, and, before
we parted, something brought me around to the subject of
the story, and I related it to him. It had the same effect
upon him that it had on me, and has had upon everybody
who has heard it, as far as I know. I think you will all agree
with me, that it is not the story itself that performs the
surgical operation on the minds of those who are familiar
with it; it is the way it is told, in print, I mean the author
has, somehow, produced a psychological effect which is
indescribable. The reader is hypnotized.He receives a
mental and moral tonic. Perhaps, doctor, you can give
some scientific explanation of the influence exerted by the
story. It is a sort of elixer manufactured out of words,
eh?''

From that the company entered upon a general
discussion of theories. Now and then slight references
were made to the story itself, and they were just sufficient
to tantalize me-the only one present who had not heard it.

At length, I left my chair, and, passing around the
table, seized Sturtevant by one arm, and succeeded in
drawing him away from the party.

"If you have any consideration for an old friend who is rapidly being driven mad by the existence of that confounded story, which Fate seems determined that I shall never hear, you will relate it to me now," I said savagely.

Sturtevant stared at me in mild surprise.

"All right," he said. "The others will excuse me for a few moments, I think. Sit down here, and you shall have it. I found it pasted in an old scrapbook I purchased in Ann Street for three cents; and there isn't a thing about it by which one can get any idea in what publication it originally appeared, or who wrote it. When I discovered it, I began casually to read it, and in a moment I was interested. Before I left it, I had read it through many times, so that I could repeat it almost word for word. It affected me strangely-as if I had come in contact with some strong personality. There seems to be in the story a personal element that applies to every one who reads it. Well, after I had read it several times, I began to think it over. I couldn't stay in the house, so I seized my coat and hat and went out. I must have walked several miles, buoyantly, without realizing that I was the same man who, only a short time before had been in the depths of despondency. That was the day I met you here, you remember."

We were interrupted at that instant by a uniformed messenger, who handed Sturtevant a telegram. It was from his chief, and demanded his instant attendance at the office. The messenger had already been delayed an hour, and there was no help for it, he must go at once.

"Too bad," said Sturtevant, rising and extending his hand. "Tell you what I'll do, old chap. I'm not likely to be gone any more than an hour or two. You take my key and wait for me in my room. In the escritoire near the window you will find an old scrapbook, bound in rawhide. It was manufactured, I have no doubt, by the author of the magic story. Wait for me in my room until I return."

With that he went out, and I lost no time in taking advantage of the permission he had given me.

I found the book with difficulty. It was a quaint, home-made affair, covered, as Sturtevant had said, with rawhide, and bound with leather throngs. The pages formed an odd combination of yellow paper, vellum and home-made parchment. I found the story, curiously printed on the last-named material. It was quaint and strange. Evidently, the printer had "set" it under the supervision of the writer. The phraseology was an unusual combination of seventeenth and eighteenth century mannerisms, and the interpolation of Italics and capitals could have originated in no other brain that that of its author.

The Magic influence of this unique story is irresistible. It contains the great secret of success for everyone. It is so skillfully and interestingly presented that a profound psychological effect is achieved in the mind of the reader.

An impression is delivered so clearly and forcefully that the reader suddenly becomes supremely aware of the great potentialities within him.

The impact of its message is so inspiring, and exhilarating that, as the final words are read an inner confidence is attained that makes no goal beyond achievement, no obstacle too great to be overcome.

Study it carefully, and you cannot fail to feel the effect that will carry you to greater happiness.

Inasmuch as I have evolved from my experience the one great secret of success for all worldly undertakings, I deem it wise, now that the number of my days is nearly counted, to give to the generations that are to follow me the benefit of whatsoever knowledge I possess. I do not apologize for the manner of my expression, nor for lack of literary merit, the latter being, I wot, its own apology. Tools much heavier than the pen have been my portion, and more-ever, the weight of years has somewhat palsied my hand and brain; nevertheless, the fact I can tell, and that I deem the meat of the nut. What mattereth it, in what manner the shell is broken, so that the meat be obtained and rendered useful? I doubt not that I shall use, in the telling, expressions that have clung to my memory since childhood; for when men attain the number of my years, to their perceptions than are events of recent happenings of youth are likely to be clearer date; nor doth it matter much how a thought is expressed, if it be wholesome and helpful, and findeth the understanding.

Much have I wearied my brain anent the questions, how best to describe this recipe for success that I have discovered, and it seemeth advisable to give it as it came to me; that is, if I relate somewhat of the story of my life, the directions for agglomerating the substances, and supplying the seasoning for the accomplishment of the dish, will plainly be perceived. Happen they may; and that men may be born generations after I am dust, who will live to bless me for the words I write.

My father, then, was a seafaring man who, early in life, forsook his vocation, and settled on a plantation in the colony of Virginia, where, some years thereafter, I was born, which event took place in the year 1642; and that was over a hundred years ago. Better for my father had it been, had he hearkened to the wise advice of my mother, that he remain in the calling of his education; but he would not have it so, and the good vessel he captained was bartered for the land I spoke of.

......**Here beginneth the first lesson to be acquired:-**

........**Man should not be blir led to whatsoever merit exists in the opportunity w' ich he hath in hand, remembering that a thousand promises for the future should weigh as naught against the possession of a single piece of silver.**

When I had achieved ten years, my mother's soul took flight, and two years thereafter my worthy father followed her. I, being their only begotten, was left alone; howbeit, there were friends who, for a time, cared for me; that is to say, they offered me a home beneath their roof, a thing which I took advantage of for the space of five months. From my father's estate there came to me naught; but in the wisdom that came with increasing years, I convinced my self that his friend under whose roof I lingered for some time, had defrauded him, and therefore me.

Of the time from age of twelve and a half until I was three and twenty, I will make no recital here, since that time hath naught to do with this tale; but some time after, having in my possesion the sum of sixteen quineas, ten, which I had saved from the fruits of my labor, I took ship to Boston town, where I began to work first as a cooper, and thereafter as a ship's carpenter, although always after craft was docked; for the sea was not amongst my desires.

Fortune will sometimes smile upon an intended victim because of pure perversity of temper. Such was one of my experiences. I prospered, and at seven and twenty, owned the yard wherein, less than four years earlier, I had worked for hire. Fortune, howbeit, is a jade who must be coerced; she will not be coddled.

......Here beginneth the second lesson to be acquired:

........Fortune is ever elusive and can only be retained by force. Deal with her tenderly and she will forsake you for a stronger man. (In that, methinks, she is not unlike other women of me knowledge.)

About this time, Disaster (which is one of the heralds of broken spirits and lost resolve,) paid me a visit. Fire ravaged my yards, leaving me nothing in its blackened paths but debts, which I had not the coin wherewith to defray. I labored with my acquaintances, seeking assistance for a new start, but the fire that had burned my competence, seemed also to have consumed their sympathies. So it happened, within a short time, that not only had I lost all, but I was hopelessly indebted to others; and for that they cast me into prison. It is possible that I might have rallied from my losses but for this last indignity, which broke down my spirits so that I became utterly despondent. Upward of a year was I detained within the goal; and when I did come forth, it was not the same hopeful, happy man, content with his lot, and with confidence in the world and its people who had entered there.

Life has many pathways, and of them by far the greater number lead downward. Some are precipitous, others are less abrupt; but ultimately, no matter at what inclination the angle may be fixed, they arrive at the same destination,-failure.

......**And here beginneth the third lesson:**

........**Failure exists only in the grave. Man, being alive, hath not yet failed; always he may turn about and ascend by the same path he descended by; (and there may be one that is less abrupt albeit longer of achievement) and more adaptable to his condition.**

When I came forth from prison, I was penniless. In all the world I possessed naught beyond the poor garment which covered me, and a walking stick which the turnkey had permitted me to retain, since it was worthless. Being a skilled workman, howbeit, I speedily found employment at good wages; but, having eaten of the fruit of worldly advantage, dissatisfaction possessed me. I became morose and sullen; whereat, to cheer my spirits, and for the sake of forgetting the losses I had sustained, I passed my evenings at the tavern. Not that I drank overmuch of liquor, except on occasion (for I have ever been somewhat abstemious), but that I could laugh and sing, and party with and badinage with my ne'er-do-well companions.

......**And here might be included the fourth lesson:**

........**Seek comrades among the industrious, for those who idle will sap your energies from you.**

It was my pleasure at that time to relate, upon slight provocation, the tale of my disasters, and to rail against the men whom I deemed to have wronged me, because they had seen fit not to come to my aid. Moreover, I found childish delight in filching from my employer, each day, a few moments of the time for which he paid me. Such a thing is less honest than downright theft.

The habit continued and grew upon me until the day dawned which found me not only without employments, but also without character, which meant that I could not hope to find work with any employer in Boston town.

It was then that I regarded myself a failure. I can liken my condition at that time for naught more similar than that of a man who, descending the steep side of a mountain, loses his foothold. The farther he slides, the faster he goes. I have also heard this condition described by the word Ishmaelite, which I understand to be a man whose hand is against everybody, and who thinks that that the hands of every other man are against him;

......And here beginneth the fifth lesson.

........The Ishmaelite and the leper are the same, since both are abominations in the sight of man,-albeit they differ much in that the former may be restored to perfect health. The former is entirely the result of imagination: The latter has poison in his blood.

I will not discourse at length upon the gradual degeneration of my energies. It is not meet ever to dwell much upon misfortunes. (which saying is also worthy of remembering.) It is enough if I add that the day came when I posessed naught wherewith to purchase food and raiment, and I found myself like unto a pauper, save at infrequent times when I could earn a few pence or mayhap a shilling. Steady employment I could not secure, so I became emaciated in body, and naught but a skeleton in spirit.

My condition, then, was deplorable; not so much for the body, be it said, as for the mental part of me, which was sick unto death. In my imagination I deemed myself ostracized by the whole world, for I had sunk very low indeed;

......**And here beginneth the sixth and final lesson; to be acquired, (which cannot be told in one sentence, nor in one paragraph, but must needs form the remainder of this tale.)**

Well do I remember my awakening, for it came in the night, when, in truth, I did awake from sleep. My bed was a pile of shavings in the rear of the cooper shop where once I had worked for for hire; my roof was the pyramid of casks, underneath which I had established myself. The night was cold, and I was chilled, albeit, paradoxically, I had been dreaming of light and warmth and of the repletion of good things. You will say, when I relate the effect the vision had on me, that my mind was affected. So be it, for it is the hope that the minds of others might be likewise influenced which disposes me to undertake the labor of this writing. It was the dream which converted me to the belief-nay, to the knowledge,-that I was possessed of two identities; and it was my own better self that afforded me the assistance for which I had pleaded in vain from my acquaintances. I have heard of the condtion described by the "double." Nevertheless, that word does not comprehend my meaning. A double can be naught more than a double, neither half being possessed of individuality. But I will not philosophize, since philosophy is naught but a suit of garments for the decoration of a dummy figure.

Moreover it was not the dream itself which affected me; it was the impression made by it, and the influence that it exerted over me, which accomplished my enfranchisement. In a word, then I encouraged my other identity. After toiling through a tempest of snow and wind, I peered into a window and saw that other being. He was rosy with health; before him, on the hearth blazed a fire of logs; there was conscious power and force in his demeanor; he was physically and mentally muscular. I rapped timidly upon the door, and he bade me enter. There was a not unkindly smile of derision in his eyes as he motioned me to a chair by the fire; but he uttered no word of welcome; and, when I had warmed myself, I went forth again into the tempest, burdened with the shame which the contrast between us had forced upon me. It was then the I awoke, and **HERE COMETH THE STRANGE PART OF MY TALE,** for when I did awake, **I WAS NOT ALONE.** There was a Presence with me; intangible to others, I discovered later, but real to me.

The Presence was in my likeness, yet was it strikingly unlike. The brow, now more lofty than my own, yet seemed more round and full; the eyes, clear, direct, and filled with purpose, glowed with enthusiasm and resolution; the lips, chin,-ay, the whole contour of face and figure was dominant and determined.

He was calm, steadfast and self-reliant; I was cowering, filled with nervous trembling, and fearsome of intangible shadows. When the Presence turned away, I followed, and throughout the day I never lost sight of it, save when it disappeared for a time beyond some doorway where I dared not enter; at such places, I awaited its return with trepidation and awe, for I could not help wondering at the temerity of the Presence (so like myself, and yet so unlike), in daring to enter where my own feet feared to tread.

It seemed also as if purposely, I was led to the place and to the man where, and before whom I most dreaded to appear; to offices where once I had transacted business; to men with whom I had financial dealings. Throughout the day I pursued the Presence, and at evening saw it disappear beyond the portals of a hostelry famous for its cheer and good living. I sought the pyramid of casks and shavings..

Not again in my dreams that night did I encounter the Better Self (for that is what I have named it), albeit, when, perchance, I awakened from slumber, it was clear to me, ever wearing that calm smile of kindly derision which could not be mistaken for pity, nor for condolence in any form. The contempt of it stung me sorely.

The second-day was not unlike the first, being a repetition of its forerunner, and I was again doomed to wait outside during the visits which the Presence paid to places where I fain would have gone had I possessed the requisite courage. It is fear which deporteth a man's soul from his body and rendereth a thing to be despised. Many a time I essayed to address it but enunciation rattled in my throat, unintelligible; and the day closed like its predecessor.

This happened many days, one following another, until I ceased to count them; albeit, I discovered that constant association with the Presence was producing an effect upon me; and one night when I awoke among the casks and discerned that he was present, I made bold to speak, albeit with marked timidity.

"Wcut

"Who are you?" I ventured to ask; and I was startled into an upright posture by the sound of my own voice; and the question seemed to give pleasure to my companion, so that I fancied there was less of derision in his smile when he responded.

"I am that I am," was the reply. "I am he who you have been; I am he who you may be again; wherefore do you hesitate? I am he who you were, and whom you have cast out for other company. I am the man made in the image of God, who once possessed your body. Once we dwelt within it together, not in harmony, for that can never be , nor yet in unity, for that is impossible, but as tenants in common who rarely fought for full possession. Then, you were a puny thing, but you became a selfish and exacting until I could not longer abide with you, therefore I stepped out. **There is a plus-entity and minus-entity in every human body that is born into the world.** Whichever one of these is favored by the flesh becomes dominant; then is the other inclined to abandon its habitation, temporarily or for all time. I am the plus-entity of yourself; you are the minus-entity. I won all things; you possess naught.

That body which we both inhabited is mine, but it is unclean, and I will not dwell within it. Cleanse it, and I will take possession."

"Why do you pursue me?" I next asked of the Presence.

"You have pursued me, not I you. You can exist without me for a time, but your path leads downward, and the end is death. Now that you approach the end, you debate if it be not politic that you should cleanse your house and invite me to enter. Step aside, then, from the brain and the will; cleanse them of your presence; only on that condition will I ever occupy them again."

"The brain has lost its power," I faltered. "The will is a weak thing; can you repair them?"

"Listen!" said the Presence, and he towered over me while I cowered abjectly at his feet. "To the plus-entity of a man, all things are possible. The world belongs to him,-is his estate. He fears naught, dreads naught, stops at naught; he asks no privileges, but demands them; he dominates, and cannot cringe; his requests are orders; opposition flees at his approach; he levels mountains, fills in vales, and travels on an even plane where stumbling is unknown."

Thereafter, I slept again, and, when I awoke, I seemed to be in a different world. The sun was shining and I was conscious that birds twittered above my head. My body, yesterday trembling and uncertain, had become vigorous and filled with energy. I gazed upon the pyramid of casks in amazement that I had so long made use of for an abiding place, and I was wonderingly conscious that I had passed my last night beneath its shelter.

The events of the night recurred to me, and I looked about me for the Presence. It was not visible, but anon I discovered, cowering in a far corner of my resting place, a puny, abject, shuddering figure, distorted of visage, deformed of shape, disheveled and unkempt of appearance. It tottered as it walked, for it approached me piteously; but I laughed aloud, mercilessly, Perchance I knew then that it was the minus-entity, and that the plus-entity was within me; albeith I did not then realize it. Moreover, I was in haste to get away; I had no time for philosophy. There was much for me to do,-much; strange it was that I had not thought of that yesterday. But yesterday was gone,-today was with me,-it had just begun.

As had once been my daily habit, I turned my steps in the direction of the tavern, where formerly I had partaken of my meals. I nodded cheerily as I entered, and smiled in recognition of returned salutations. Men who had ignored me for months bowed graciously when I passed them on the thorough-fare. I went to the washroom, and from there to the breakfast table; afterwards when I passed the taproom, I paused a moment and said to the landlord:

"I will occupy the same room that I formerly used, if perchance, you have it at disposal. If not, another will do as well, until I can obtain it."

Then I went out and hurried with all haste to the cooperage. There was a huge wain in the yard, and men were loading it with casks for shipment. I asked no questions, but, seizing barrels, began hurling them to the men who worked atop of the load. When this was finished, I entered the shop. There was a vacant bench; I recognized its disuse by the litter on its top. It was the same at which I had once worked. Stripping off my coat, I soon cleared it of impedimenta. In a moment more I was seated, with my foot on the vice-lever, shaving staves.

"It was an hour later when the master workmen entered the room, and he paused in surprise at sight of me; already there was a goodly pile of neatly shaven staves beside me, for in those days I was an excellent workmen; there was none better, but, alas! now, age hath deprived me of my skill. I replied to his unasked question with the brief, but comprehensive sentence: "I have returned to work sir." He nodded his head and passed on, viewing the work of other men, albeith anon he glanced askance in my direction.

Here endeth the sixth and last lesson to be aquired, although there is more to be said since from that moment I was a successful man, and ere long possessed another shipyard, and had aquired a full competence of wordly goods.

I pray you who read, heed well the following admonitions, since upon them depend the word "success" and all that it implies:

Whatsoever you desire of good is yours. You have but to stretch forth your hand and take it.

....I pray you who read, heed well the following admonitions, since upon them depend the word "success" and all that it implies:

......Whatsoever you desire of good is yours. You have but to streth forth your hand and take it.

......Learn that the consciousness of dominant power within you is the possession of all things attainable.

......Have no fear of any sort or shape, for fear is an adjunct of the minus-entity.

......If you have skill, apply it; the world must profil by it, and therefore, you.

......Make a daily and nightly companion of your plus - entity; if you heed its advice, you cannot go wrong.

......Go, therefore, and do that which is within you to do; take no heed of gestures which would beckon you aside; ask of no man permission to perform.

......The minus-entity requests favors; the plus entity grants them. Fortune waits upon every footstep you take; seize her, bind her, hold her, for she is yours; she belongs to you.

......Start out now, with these admonisions in your mind. Stretch out your hand, and grasp the plus which, maybe, you have never made use of save in great emergencies. Life is an emergency most grave.

......Your plus-entity is beside you now: cleanse your brain, and strengthen your will. It will take possession. It waits upon you.

......Be always on your guard. Whichever entity controls you, the other hovers at your side; beware lest the evil enter, even for a moment.

......My task is done. I have written the recipe for "success." If followed, it cannot fail. Wherein I may not be entirely comprehended, the plus-entity of whosoever read will supply the deficiency; and upon that Better Self of mine, I place the burden of imparting to generations that are to come, the secret of this all-pervading good,-

....The secret of being what you have it within you to be.

AS A MAN THINKETH

This little volume (the result of meditation and experience) is not intended as an exhaustive treatise on the much-written-upon subject of the power of thought. It is suggestive rather than explanatory, its object being to stimulate men and women to the discovery and perception of the truth that—

"They themselves are makers of themselves"

by virtue of the thoughts which they choose and encourage; that mind is the master weaver, both of the inner garment of character and the outer garment of circumstance, and that, as they may have hitherto woven in ignorance and pain they may now weave in enlightenment and happiness.

James Allen

BROAD PARK AVENUE,
  ILFRACOMBE,
    ENGLAND.

THOUGHT AND CHARACTER

The aphorism, "As a man thinketh in his heart so is he," not only embraces the whole of a man's being, but is so comprehensive as to reach out to every condition and circumstance of his life. A man is literally **what he thinks**, his character being the complete sum of all his thoughts.

As the plant springs from, and could not be without, the seed, so every act of a man springs from the hidden seeds of thought, and could not have appeared without them. This applies equally to those acts called "spontaneous" and "unpremeditated" as to those which are deliberately executed.

Act is the blossom of thought, and joy and suffering are its fruits; thus does a man garner in the sweet and bitter fruitage of his own husbandry.

> "Thought in the mind hath made us. What we are
> By thought was wrought and built. If a man's mind
> Hath evil thoughts, pain comes on him as comes
> The wheel the ox behind. . . .
> . . . If one endure
> In purity of thought, joy follows him
> As his own shadow—sure."

Man is a growth by law, and not a creation by artifice, and cause and effect is as absolute and undeviating in the hidden realm of thought as in the world of visible and material things. A noble and Godlike character is not a thing of favour or chance, but is the natural result of continued effort in right thinking, the effect of long-cherished association with Godlike thoughts. An ignoble and bestial character, by the same process, is the result of the continued harbouring of grovelling thoughts.

Man is made or unmade by himself; in the armoury of thought he forges the weapons by which he destroys himself; he also fashions the tools with which he builds for himself heavenly mansions of joy and strength and peace.

By the right choice and true application of thought, man ascends to the Divine Perfection; by the abuse and wrong application of thought, he descends below the level of the beast. Between these two extremes are all the grades of character, and man is their maker and master.

Of all the beautiful truths pertaining to the soul which have been restored and brought to light in this age, none is more gladdening or fruitful of divine promise and confidence than this—that man is the master of thought, the moulder of character, and the maker and shaper of condition, environment, and destiny.

As a being of Power, Intelligence, and Love, and the lord of his own thoughts, man holds the key to every situation, and contains within himself that transforming and regenerative agency by which he may make himself what he wills.

Man is always the master, even in his weakest and most abandoned state; but in his weakness and degradation he is the foolish master who misgoverns his "household." When he begins to reflect upon his condition, and to search diligently for the Law upon which his being is established, he then becomes the wise master, directing his energies with intelligence, and fashioning his thoughts to fruitful issues. Such is the **conscious** master, and man can only thus become by discovering **within himself** the laws of thought; which discovery is totally a matter of application, self-analysis, and experience.

Only by much searching and mining are gold and diamonds obtained, and man can find every truth connected with his being if he will dig deep into the mine of his soul; and that he is the maker of his character, the moulder of his life, and the builder of his destiny, he may unerringly prove, if he will watch, control, and alter his thoughts, tracing their effects upon himself, upon others, and upon his life and circumstances. linking cause and effect by patient practice and investigation, and utilising his every experience, even to the most trivial, everyday occurrence, as a means of obtaining that knowledge of himself which is Understanding, Wisdom, Power. In this direction, as in no other, is the law absolute that "He that seeketh findeth; and to him that knocketh it shall be opened"; for only by patience, practice, and ceaseless importunity can a man enter the Door of the Temple of Knowledge.

EFFECT OF THOUGHT ON CIRCUMSTANCES

A man's mind may be likened to a garden, which may be intelligently cultivated or allowed to run wild; but whether cultivated or neglected, it must, and will, **bring forth.** If no useful seeds are **put** into it, then an abundance of useless weed seeds will **fall** therein, and will continue to produce their kind.

Just as a gardener cultivates his plot, keeping it free from weeds, and growing the flowers and fruits which he requires, so may a man tend the garden of his mind, weeding out all the wrong, useless, and impure thoughts, and cultivating toward perfection the flowers and fruits of right, useful, and pure thoughts. By pursuing this process, a man sooner or later discovers that he is the master gardener of his soul, the director of his life. He also reveals, within himself, the laws of thought, and understands, with ever-increasing accuracy, how the thought forces and mind elements operate in the shaping of his character, circumstances, and destiny.

Thought and character are one, and as character can only manifest and discover itself through environment and circumstance, the outer conditions of a person's life will always be found to be harmoniously related to his inner state. This does not mean that a man's circumstances at any given time are an indication of his **entire** character, but that those circumstances are so intimately connected with some vital thought element within himself that, for the time being, they are indispensable to his development.

Every man is where he is by the law of his being; the thoughts which he has built into his character have brought him there, and in the arrangement of his life there is no element of chance, but all is the result of a law which cannot err. This is just as true of those who feel "out of harmony" with their surroundings as of those who are contented with them.

As a progressive and evolving being, man is where he is that he may learn that he may grow; and as he learns the spiritual lesson which any circumstance contains for him, it passes away and gives place to other circumstances.

Man is buffeted by circumstances so long as he believes himself to be the creature of outside conditions, but when he realises that he is a creative power, and that he may command the hidden soil and seeds of his being out of which circumstances grow, he then becomes the rightful master of himself.

That circumstances **grow** out of thought every man knows who has for any length of time practised self-control and self-purification, for he will have noticed that the alteration in his circumstances has been in exact ratio with his altered mental condition. So true is this that when a man earnestly applies himself to remedy the defects in his character, and makes swift and marked progress, he passes rapidly through a succession of vicissitudes.

The soul attracts that which it secretly harbours; that which it loves, and also that which it fears; it reaches the height of its cherished aspirations; it falls to the level of its unchastened desires—and circumstances are the means by which the soul receives its own.

Every thought seed sown or allowed to fall into the mind, and to take root there, produces its own, blossoming sooner or later into act, and bearing its own fruitage of opportunity and circumstance. Good thoughts bear good fruit, bad thoughts bad fruit.

The outer world of circumstance shapes itself to the
inner world of thought, and both pleasant and unpleasant
external conditions are factors which make for the
ultimate good of the individual. As the reaper of his own
harvest, man learns both by suffering and bliss.

Following the inmost desires, aspirations, thoughts, by
which he allows himself to be dominated (pursuing the
will-o'-the-wisps of impure imaginings or steadfastly
walking the highway of strong and high endeavour), a man
at last arrives at their fruition and fulfilment in the outer
conditions of his life. The laws of growth and adjustment
everywhere obtain.

A man does not come to the almshouse or the jail by the
tyranny of fate or circumstance, but by the pathway of
grovelling thoughts and base desires. Nor does a pure-
minded man fall suddenly into crime by stress of any mere
external force; the criminal thought had long been
secretly fostered in the heart, and the hour of opportunity
revealed its gathered power. Circumstance does not make
the man; it reveals him to himself. No such conditions can
exist as descending into vice and its attendant sufferings
apart from vicious inclinations, or ascending into virtue
and its pure happiness without the continued cultivation of
virtuous aspirations; and man, therefore, as the lord and
master of thought, is the maker of himself, the shaper and
author of environment. Even at birth the soul comes to its
own, and through every step of its earthly pilgrimage it
attracts those combinations of conditions which reveal
itself, which are the reflections of its own purity and impurity, its strength and weakness.

Men do not attract that which they **want,** but that which
they **are.** Their whims, fancies, and ambitions are th-
warted at every step, but their inmost thoughts and desires
are fed with their own food, be it foul or clean. The
"divinity that shapes our ends" is in ourselves; it is our
very self. Man is manacled only by himself: thought and
action are the jailers of Fate—they imprison, being base;

they are also the angels of Freedom—they liberate, being noble. Not what he wishes and prays for does a man get, but what he justly earns. His wishes and prayers are only gratified and answered when they harmonise with his thoughts and actions.

In the light of this truth, what, then, is the meaning of "fighting against circumstances"? It means that a man is continually revolting against an **effect** without, while all the time he is nourishing and preserving its **cause** in his heart. That cause may take the form of a conscious vice or an unconscious weakness; but whatever it is, it stubbornly retards the efforts of its possessor, and thus calls aloud for remedy.

Men are anxious to improve their circumstances, but are unwilling to improve themselves; they therefore remain bound. The man who does not shrink from self-crucifixion can never fail to accomplish the object upon which his heart is set. This is as true of earthly as of heavenly things. Even the man whose sole object is to acquire wealth must be prepared to make great personal sacrifices before he can accomplish his object; and how much more so he who would realise a strong and well-poised life?

Here is a man who is wretchedly poor. He is extremely anxious that his surroundings and home comforts should be improved, yet all the time he shirks his work, and considers he is justified in trying to deceive his employer on the ground of the insufficiency of his wages. Such a man does not understand the simplest rudiments of those principles which are the basis of true prosperity, and is not only totally unfitted to rise out of his wretchedness, but is actually attracting to himself a still deeper wretchedness by dwelling in and acting out, indolent, deceptive, and unmanly thoughts.

Here is a rich man who is the victim of a painful and persistent disease as the result of gluttony. He is willing to give large sums of money to get rid of it, but he will not sacrifice his gluttonous desires. He wants to gratify his taste for rich and unnatural viands and have his health as well. Such a man is totally unfit to have health, because he has not yet learned the first principles of a healthy life.

Here is an employer of labour who adopts crooked measures to avoid paying the regulation wage, and, in the hope of making larger profits, reduces the wages of his work-people. Such a man is altogether unfitted for prosperity, and when he finds himself bankrupt, both as regards reputation and riches, he blames circumstances, not knowing that he is the sole author of his condition.

I have introduced these three cases merely as illustrative of the truth that man is the causer (though nearly always unconsciously) of his circumstances, and that, while aiming at a good end, he is continually frustrating its accomplishment by encouraging thoughts and desires which cannot possibly harmonise with that end. Such cases could be multiplied and varied almost indefinitely, but this is not necessary, as the reader can, if he so resolves, trace the action of the laws of thought in his own mind and life, and until this is done, mere external facts cannot serve as a ground of reasoning.

Circumstances, however, are so complicated, thought is so deeply rooted, and the conditions of happiness vary so vastly with individuals, that a man's **entire** soul condition (although it may be known to himself) cannot be judged by another from the external aspect of his life alone. A man may be honest in certain directio is, yet suffer privations; a man may be dishonest in certa n directions, yet acquire wealth; but the conclusion usually formed that the one man fails **because of his particular honesty,** and that the other prospers **because of his particular dishonesty,** is the result of a superficial judgment, which assumes that the dishonest man is almost totally corrupt, and the honest man almost entirely virtuous. In the light of a deeper knowledge and wider experience, such judgment is found to be erroneous. The dishonest man may have some admirable virtues which the other does not possess; and the honest man obnoxious vices which are absent in the other. The honest man reaps the good results of his honest thoughts and acts; he also brings upon himself the sufferings which his vices produce. The dishonest man likewise garners his own suffering and happiness.

It is pleasing to human vanity to believe that one suffers because of one's virtue; but not until a man has extirpated every sickly, bitter, and impure thought from his mind, and washed every sinful stain from his soul, can he be in a position to know and declare that his sufferings are the result of his good, and not of his bad qualities; and on the way to, yet long before he has reached, that supreme perfection, he will have found, working in his mind and life, the Great Law which is absolutely just, and which cannot, therefore, give good for evil, evil for good Possessed of such knowledge, he will then know, looking back upon his past ignorance and blindness, that his life is, and always was, justly ordered, and that all his past experiences, good and bad, were the equitable outworking of his evolving, yet unevolved self.

Good thoughts and actions can never produce bad results; bad thoughts and actions can never produce good results. This is but saying that nothing can come from corn but corn, nothing from nettles but nettles. Men understand this law in the natural world, and work with it; but few understand it in the mental and moral world (though its operation there is just as simple and undeviating), and they, therefore, do not co-operate with it.

Suffering is always the effect of wrong thought in some direction. It is an indication that the individual is out of harmony with himself, with the Law of his being. The sole and supreme use of suffering is to purify, to burn out all that is useless and impure. Suffering ceases for him who is pure. There could be no object in burning gold after the dross had been removed, and a perfectly pure and enlightened being could not suffer.

The circumstances which a man encounters with suffering are the result of his own mental inharmony. The circumstances which a man encounters with blessedness are the result of his own mental harmony. Blessedness, not material possessions, is the measure of right thought; wretchedness, not lack of material possessions, is the measure of wrong thought. A man may be cursed and rich; he may be blessed and poor. Blessedness and riches are only joined together when the riches are rightly and wisely used; and the poor man only descends into wretchedness when he regards his lot as a burden unjustly imposed.

Indigence and indulgence are the two extremes of wretchedness. They are both equally unnatural and the result of mental disorder. A man is not rightly conditioned until he is a happy, healthy, and prosperous being; and happiness, health, and prosperity are the result of a harmonious adjustment of the inner with the outer, of the man with his surroundings.

A man only begins to be a man when he ceases to whine and revile, and commences to search for the hidden justice which regulates his life. And as he adapts his mind to that regulating factor, he ceases to accuse others as the cause of his condition, and builds himself up in strong and noble thoughts; ceases to kick against circumstances, but begins to use them as aids to his more rapid progress, and as a means of discovering the hidden powers and possibilities within himself.

Law, not confusion, is the dominating principle in the universe; justice, not injustice, is the soul and substance of life; and righteousness, not corruption, is the moulding and moving force in the spiritual government of the world. This being so, man has but to right himself to find that the universe is right; and during the process of putting himself right, he will find that as he alters his thoughts toward things, and other people, things and other people will alter toward him.

The proof of this truth is in every person, and it therefore admits of easy investigation by systematic introspection and self-analysis. Let a man radically alter his thoughts, and he will be astonished at the rapid transformation it will effect in the material conditions of his life. Men imagine that thought can be kept secret, but it cannot; it rapidly crystallises into habit, and habit solidifies into circumstance. Bestial thoughts crystallise into habits of drunkenness and sensuality, which solidify into circumstances of destitution and disease: impure thoughts of every kind crystallise into enervating and confusing habits, which solidify into distracting and adverse circumstances; thoughts of fear, doubt, and indecision crystallise into weak, unmanly, and irresolute habits, which solidify into circumstances of failure, indigence, and slavish dependence: lazy thoughts crystallise into habits of uncleanliness and dishonesty, which solidify into circumstances of foulness and beggary: hateful and condemnatory thoughts crystallise into habits of accusation and violence, which solidify into circumstances of injury and persecution: selfish thoughts of all kinds crystallise into habits of self-seeking, which solidify into circumstances more or less distressing. On the other hand, beautiful thoughts of all kinds crystallise into habits of grace and kindliness, which solidify into genial and sunny circumstances: pure thoughts crystallise into habits of temperance and self-control, which solidify into circumstances of repose and peace: thoughts of courage, self-reliance, and decision crystallise into manly habits, which solidify into circumstances of success, plenty, and freedom: energetic thoughts crystallise into habits of cleanliness and industry, which solidify into circumstances of pleasantness: gentle and forgiving thoughts crystallise into habits of gentleness, which solidify into protective and preservative circumstances: loving and unselfish thoughts crystallise into habits of self-forgetfulness for others, which solidify into circumstances of sure and abiding prosperity and true riches.

A particular train of thought persisted in, be it good or
bad, cannot fail to produce its results on the character and
circumstances. A man cannot **directly** choose his circumstances, but he can choose his thoughts, and so indirectly, yet surely, shape his circumstances.

Nature helps every man to the gratification of the
thoughts which he most encourages, and opportunities are
presented which will most speedily bring to the surface
both the good and evil thoughts.

Let a man cease from his sinful thoughts, and all the
world will soften toward him, and be ready to help him; let
him put away his weakly and sickly thoughts, and lo!
opportunities will spring up on every hand to aid his strong
resolves; let him encourage good thoughts, and no hard
fate shall bind him down to wretchedness and shame. The
world is your kaleidoscope, and the varying combinations
of colours which at every succeeding moment it presents
to you are the exquisitely adjusted pictures of your ever-
moving thoughts.

"You will be what you will be;
  Let failure find its false content
  In that poor word, 'environment,'
But spirit scorns it, and is free.

"It masters time, it conquers space;
  It cowes that boastful trickster, Chance,
  And bids the tyrant Circumstance
Uncrown, and fill a servant's place.

"The human Will, that force unseen,
  The offspring of a deathless Soul,
  Can hew a way to any goal,
Though walls of granite intervene.

"Be not impatient in delay,
  But wait as one who understands;
  When spirit rises and commands,
The gods are ready to obey."

EFFECT OF THOUGHT ON
HEALTH AND THE BODY

The body is the servant of the mind. It obeys the operations of the mind, whether they be deliberately chosen or automatically expressed. At the bidding of unlawful thoughts the body sinks rapidly into disease and decay; at the command of glad and beautiful thoughts it becomes clothed with youthfulness and beauty.

Disease and health, like circumstances, are rooted in thought. Sickly thoughts will express themselves through a sickly body. Thoughts of fear have been known to kill a man as speedily as a bullet, and they are continually killing thousands of people just as surely though less rapidly. The people who live in fear of disease are the people who get it. Anxiety quickly demoralises the whole body, and lays it open to the entrance of disease; while impure thoughts, even if not physically indulged, will soon shatter the nervous system.

Strong, pure, and happy thoughts build up the body in vigour and grace. The body is a delicate and plastic instrument, which responds readily to the thoughts by which it is impressed, and habits of thought will produce their own effects, good or bad, upon it.

Men will continue to have impure and poisoned blood so long as they propagate unclean thoughts. Out of a clean heart comes a clean life and a clean body. Out of a defiled mind proceeds a defiled life and a corrupt body. Thought is the fount of action, life, and manifestation; make the fountain pure, and all will be pure.

Change of diet will not help a man who will not change his thoughts. When a man makes his thoughts pure, he no longer desires impure food.

Clean thoughts make clean habits. The so-called saint who does not wash his body is not a saint. He who has strengthened and purified his thoughts does not need to consider the malevolent microbe.

If you would perfect your body, guard your mind. If you would renew your body, beautify your mind. Thoughts of malice, envy, disappointment, despondency, rob the body of its health and grace. A sour face does not come by chance; it is made by sour thoughts. Wrinkles that mar are drawn by folly, passion, pride.

I know a woman of ninety-six who has the bright, innocent face of a girl. I know a man well under middle age whose face is drawn into inharmonious contours. The one is the result of a sweet and sunny disposition; the other is the outcome of passion and discontent.

As you cannot have a sweet and wholesome abode unless you admit the air and sunshine freely into your rooms, so a strong body and a bright, happy, or serene countenance can only result from the free admittance into the mind of thoughts of joy and good will and serenity.

On the faces of the aged there are wrinkles made by sympathy; others by strong and pure thought, and others are carved by passion: who cannot distinguish them? With those who have lived righteously, age is calm, peaceful, and softly mellowed, like the setting sun. I have recently seen a philosopher on his deathbed. He died as sweetly and peacefully as he had lived.

There is no physician like cheerful thought for dissipating the ills of the body; there is no comforter to compare with good will for dispersing the shadows of grief and sorrow. To live continually in thoughts of ill will, cynicism, suspicion, and envy, is to be confined in a self-made prison hole. But to think well of all, to be cheerful with all, to patiently learn to find the good in all—such unselfish thoughts are the very portals of heaven; and to dwell day by day in thoughts of peace toward every creature will bring abounding peace to their possessor.

THOUGHT AND PURPOSE

Until thought is linked with purpose there is no intelligent accomplishment. With the majority the bark of thought is allowed to "drift" upon the ocean of life. Aimlessness is a vice, and such drifting must not continue for him who would steer clear of catastrophe and destruction.

They who have no central purpose in their life fall an easy prey to petty worries, fears, troubles, and self-pityings, all of which are indications of weakness, which lead, just as surely as deliberately planned sins (though by a different route), to failure, unhappiness, and loss, for weakness cannot persist in a power-evolving universe.

A man should conceive of a legitimate purpose in his heart, and set out to accomplish it. He should make this purpose the centralising point of his thoughts. It may take the form of a spiritual ideal, or it may be a worldly object, according to his nature at the time being; but whichever it is, he should steadily focus his thought forces upon the object which he has set before him. He should make this purpose his supreme duty, and should devote himself to its attainment, not allowing his thoughts to wander away into ephemeral fancies, longings, and imaginings. This is the royal road to self-control and true concentration of thought. Even if he fails again and again to accomplish his purpose (as he necessarily must until weakness is overcome), the **strength of character gained** will be the measure of his **true** success, and this will form a new starting point for future power and triumph.

Those who are not prepared for the apprehension of a great purpose, should fix the thoughts upon the faultless performance of their duty, no matter how insignificant their task may appear. Only in this way can the thoughts be gathered and focussed, and resolution and energy be developed, which being done, there is nothing which may not be accomplished.

The weakest soul, knowing its own weakness, and believing this truth—that strength can only be developed by effort and practice, will, thus believing, at once begin to exert itself, and, adding effort to effort, patience to patience, and strength to strength, will never cease to develop, and will at last grow divinely strong.

As the physically weak man can make himself strong by careful and patient training, so the man of weak thoughts can make them strong by exercising himself in right thinking.

To put away aimlessness and weakness, and to begin to think with purpose, is to enter the ranks of those strong ones who only recognise failure as one of the pathways to attainment; who make all conditions serve them, and who think strongly, attempt fearlessly, and accomplish masterfully.

Having conceived of his purpose, a man should mentally mark out a straight pathway to its achievement, looking neither to the right not the left. Doubts and fears should be rigorously excluded; they are disintegrating elements which break up the straight line of effort, rendering it crooked, ineffectual, useless. Thoughts of doubt and fear never accomplish anything, and never can. They always lead to failure. Purpose, energy, power to do, and all strong thoughts cease when doubt and fear creep in.

The will to do springs from the knowledge that we cando. Doubt and fear are the great enemies of knowledge, and he who encourages them, who does not slay them, thwarts himself at every step.

He who has conquered doubt and fear has conquered failure. His every thought is allied with power, and all difficulties are bravely met and wisely overcome. His purposes are seasonably planted, and they bloom and bring forth fruit which does not fall prematurely to the ground.

Thought allied fearlessly to purpose becomes creative force: he who **knows** this is ready to become something higher and stronger than a mere bundle of wavering thoughts and fluctuating sensations; he who **does** this has become the conscious and intelligent wielder of his mental powers.

THE THOUGHT-FACTOR IN
ACHIEVEMENT

All that a man achieves and all that he fails to achieve is the direct result of his own thoughts. In a justly ordered universe, where loss of equipoise would mean total destruction, individual responsibility must be absolute. A man's weakness and strength, purity and impurity, are his own, and not another man's; they are brought about by himself, and not by another; and they can only be altered by himself, never by another. His condition is also his own, and not another man's. His suffering and his happiness are evolved from within. As he thinks, so he is; as he continues to think, so he remains.

A strong man cannot help a weaker unless that weaker is **willing** to be helped, and even then the weak man must become strong of himself; he must, by his own efforts, develop the strength which he admires in another. None but himself can alter his condition.

It has been usual for men to think and to say, "Many men are slaves because one is an oppressor; let us hate the oppressor." Now, however, there is among an increasing few a tendency to reverse this judgment, and to say, "One man is an oppressor because many are slaves; let us despise the slaves." The truth is that oppressor and slave are co-operators in ignorance, and, while seeming to afflict each other, are in reality afflicting themselves. A perfect Knowledge perceives the action of law in the weakness of the oppressed and the misapplied power of the oppressor; a perfect Love, seeing the suffering which both states entail, condemns neither; a perfect Compassion embraces both oppressor and oppressed.

He who has conquered weakness, and has put away all selfish thoughts, belongs neither to oppressor nor oppressed. He is free.

A man can only rise, conquer, and achieve by lifting up his thoughts. He can only remain weak, and abject, and miserable by refusing to lift up his thoughts.

Before a man can achieve anything, even in worldly things, he must lift his thoughts above slavish animal indulgence. He may not, in order to succeed, give up **all** animality and selfishness, by any means; but a portion of it must, at least, be sacrificed. A man whose first thought is bestial indulgence could neither think clearly nor plan methodically; he could not find and develop his latent resources, and would fail in any undertaking. Not having commenced manfully to control his thought, he is not in a position to control affairs and to adopt serious responsibilities. He is not fit to act independently and stand alone. But he is limited only by the thoughts which he chooses.

There can be no progress, no achievement without sacrifice, and a man's worldly success will be in the measure that he sacrifices his confused animal thoughts, and fixes his mind on the development of his plans, and the strengthening of his resolution and self-reliance. And the higher he lifts his thoughts, the more manly, upright, and righteous he becomes, the greater will be his success, the more blessed and enduring will be his achievements.

The universe does not favour the greedy, the dishonest, the vicious, although on the mere surface it may sometimes appear to do so; it helps the honest, the magnanimous, the virtuous. All the great Teachers of the ages have declared this in varying forms, and to prove and know it a man has but to persist in making himself more and more virtuous by lifting up his thoughts.

Intellectual achievements are the result of thought consecrated to the search for knowledge, or for the beautiful and true in life and nature. Such achievements may be sometimes connected with vanity and ambition, but they are not the outcome of those characteristics; they are the natural outgrowth of long and arduous effort, and of pure and unselfish thoughts.

Spiritual achievements are the consummation of holy aspirations. He who lives constantly in the conception of noble and lofty thoughts, who dwells upon all that is pure and unselfish, will, as surely as the sun reaches its zenith and the moon its full, become wise and noble in character, and rise into a position of influence and blessedness.

Achievement, of whatever kind, is the crown of effort, the diadem of thought. By the aid of self-control, resolution, purity, righteousness, and well-directed thought a man ascends; by the aid of animality, indolence, impurity, corruption, and confusion of thought a man descends.

A man may rise to high success in the world, and even to lofty altitudes in the spiritual realm, and again descend into weakness and wretchedness by allowing arrogant, selfish, and corrupt thoughts to take possession of him.

Victories attained by right thought can only be maintained by watchfulness. Many give way when success is assured, and rapidly fall back into failure.

All achievements, whether in the business, intellectual, or spiritual world, are the result of definitely directed thought, are governed by the same law and are of the same method; the only difference lies in **the object of attainment.**

He who would accomplish little must sacrifice little; he who would achieve much must sacrifice much; he who would attain highly must sacrifice greatly.

VISIONS AND IDEALS

The dreamers are the saviours of the world. As the visible world is sustained by the invisible, so man, through all their trials and sins and sordid vocations, are nourished by the beautiful visions of their solitary dreamers. Humanity cannot forget its dreamers; it cannot let their ideals fade and die; it lives in them; it knows them as the realities which it shall one day see and know.

Composer, sculptor, painter, poet, prophet, sage, these are the makers of the afterworld, the architects of heaven. The world is beautiful because they have lived; without them, labouring humanity would perish.

He who cherishes a beautiful vision, a lofty ideal in his heart, will one day realize it. Columbus cherished a vision of another world, and he discovered it; Copernicus fostered the vision of a multiplicity of worlds and a wider universe, and he revealed it; Buddha beheld the vision of a spiritual world of stainless beauty and perfect peace, and he entered into it.

Cherish your visions; cherish your ideals; cherish the music that stirs in your heart, the beauty that forms in your mind, the loveliness that drapes your purest thoughts, for out of them will grow all delightful conditions, all heavenly environment; of these, if you but remain true to them, your world will at last be built.

To desire is to obtain; to aspire is to achieve. Shall man's basest desires receive the fullest measure of gratification, and his purest aspirations starve for lack of sustenance? Such is not the Law: such a condition of things can never obtain: "Ask and receive."

Dream lofty dreams, and as you dream, so shall you become. Your Vision is the promise of what you shall one day be; your Ideal is the property of what you shall at last unveil.

The greatest achievement was at first and for a time a dream. The oak sleeps in the acorn; the bird waits in the egg; and in the highest vision of the soul a waking angel stirs. Dreams are the seedlings of realities.

Your circumstances may be uncongenial, but they shall not long remain so if you but perceive an Ideal and strive to reach it. You cannot travel **within** and stand still **without**. Here is a youth hard pressed by poverty and labour; confined long hours in an unhealthy workshop; unschooled, and lacking all the arts of refinement. But he dreams of better things; he thinks of intelligence, of refinement, of grace and beauty. He conceives of, mentally builds up, an ideal condition of life; the vision of a wider liberty and a larger scope takes possession of him; unrest urges him to action, and he utilises all his spare time and means, small though they are, to the development of his latent powers and resources. Very soon so altered has his mind become that the workshop can no longer hold him. It has become so out of harmony with his mentality that it falls out of his life as a garment is cast aside, and, with the growth of opportunities which fit the scope of his expanding powers, he passes out of it forever. Years later we see this youth as a full-grown man. We find him a master of certain forces of the mind which he wields with world-wide influence and almost unequalled power. In his hands he holds the cords of gigantic responsibilities; he speaks, and lo! lives are changed; men and women hang upon his words and remould their characters, and, sunlike, he becomes the fixed and luminous center around which innumerable destinies revolve. He has realised the Vision of his youth. He has become one with his Ideal.

And you, too, youthful reader, will realise the Vision (not the idle wish) of your heart, be it base or beautiful, or a mixture of both, for you will always gravitate toward that which you, secretly, most love. Into your hands will be placed the exact results of your own thoughts; you will receive that which you earn; no more, no less. Whatever your present environment may be, you will fall, remain, or rise with your thoughts, your Vision, your ideal. You will

become as small as your controlling desire; as great as
your dominant aspiration: in the beautiful words of
Stanton Kirkham Davis, "You may be keeping accounts,
and presently you shall walk out of the door that for so long
has seemed to you the barrier of your ideals, and shall find
yourself before an audience—the pen still behind your ear,
the ink stains on your fingers—and then and there shall
pour out the torrent of your inspiration. You may be
driving sheep, and you shall wander to the city—bucolic
and open mouthed; shall wander under the intrepid
guidance of the spirit into the studio of the master, and
after a time he shall say, 'I have nothing more to teach
you.' And now you have become the master, who did so
recently dream of great things while driving sheep. You
shall lay down the saw and the plane to take upon yourself
the regeneration of the world."

The thoughtless, the ignorant, and the indolent, seeing
only the apparent effects of things and not the things
themselves, talk of luck, of fortune, and chance. Seeing a
man grow rich, they say, "How lucky he is!" Observing
another become intellectual, they exclaim, "How highly
favoured he is!" And noting the saintly character and wide
influence of another, they remark, "How chance aids him
at every turn!" They do not see the trials and failures and
struggles which these men have voluntarily encountered
in order to gain their experience; have no knowledge of the
sacrifices they have made, of the undaunted efforts they
have put forth, of the faith they have exercised, that they
might overcome the apparently insurmountable, and
realise the Vision of their heart. They do not know the
darkness and the heartaches; they only see the light and
joy, and call it "luck"; do not see the long and arduous
journey, but only behold the pleasant goal, and call it
"good fortune"; do not understand the process, but only
perceive the result, and call it "chance."

In all human affairs there are **efforts**, and there are
results, and the strength of the effort is the measure of the

result. Chance is not. "Gifts," powers, material, intellectual, and spiritual possessions are the frutis of effort; they are thoughts completed, objects accomplished, visions realized.

The Vision that you glorify in your mind, the Ideal that you enthrone in your heart—this you will build your life by, this you will become.

SERENITY

Calmness of mind is one of the beautiful jewels of wisdom. It is the result of long and patient effort in self-control. Its presence is an indication of ripened experience, and of a more than ordinary knowledge of the laws and operations of thought.

A man becomes calm in the measure that he understands himself as a thought-evolved being, for such knowledge necessitates the understanding of others as the result of thought, and as he develops a right understanding, and sees more and more clearly the internal relations of things by the action of cause and effect, he ceases to fuss and fume and worry and grieve, and remains poised, steadfast, serene.

The calm man, having learned how to govern himself, knows how to adapt himself to others; and they, in turn, reverence his spiritual strength, and feel that they can learn of him and rely upon him. The more tranquil a man becomes, the greater is his success, his influence, his power for good. Even the ordinary trader will find his business prosperity increase as he develops a greater self-control and equanimity, for people will always prefer to deal with a man whose demeanour is strongly equable.

The strong, calm man is always loved and revered. He is like a shade-giving tree in a thirsty land, or a sheltering rock in a storm. "Who does not love a tranquil heart, a sweet-tempered, balanced life? It does not matter whether it rains or shines, or what changes come to those possessing these blessings, for they are always sweet, serene, and calm. That exquisite poise of character which we call serenity is the last lesson of culture; it is the flowering of life, the fruitage of the soul. It is precious as wisdom, more to be desired than gold—yea, than even fine gold. How insignificant mere money-seeking looks in comparison with a serene life—a life that dwells in the ocean of Truth, beneath the waves, beyond the reach of tempests, in the Eternal Calm!

"How many people we know who sour their lives, who ruin all that is sweet and beautiful by explosive tempers, who destroy their poise of character, and make bad blood! It is a question whether the great majority of people do not ruin their lives and mar their happiness by lack of self-control. How few people we meet in life who are well-balanced, who have that exquisite poise which is characteristic of the finished character!"

Yes, humanity surges with uncontrolled passion, is tumultuous with ungoverned grief, is blown about by anxiety and doubt. Only the wise man, only he whose thoughts are controlled and purified, makes the winds and the storms of the soul obey him.

Tempest-tossed souls, wherever ye may be, under whatsoever conditions ye may live, know this—in the ocean of life the isles of Blessedness are smiling, and the sunny shore of your ideal awaits your coming. Keep your hand firmly upon the helm of thought. In the back of your soul reclines the commanding Master; He does but sleep; wake Him. Self-control is strength; Right Thought is mastery; Calmness is power. Say unto your heart, "Peace, be still!"

ACRES OF DIAMONDS

Russells Conwell's **Acres of Diamonds** may be the most famous bit of speechmaking in the history of the American lecture platform; it is certainly one of the most enduring. And it is as pertinent and inspiring today as it was the first time he delivered it, near the turn of the century.

The fame of the lecture may be tied up with the method and spirit of the lecturer. Conwell had a unique method. He would arrive in the town in which he was to lecture, as early as possible; he would visit the postmaster, the school principal, the ministers, the factory workers at their benches, and ring a few doorbells to talk with the local housewives. That was done that he might find out something about the town-its history, its people ("what opportunities they had, and what they had failed to do"), and then he would get up on the rostrum and point to the acres of diamonds in their own back yards. It never failed.

People loved him more than his lecture. In his last days as pastor of famed Baptist Temple in Philadelphia, he would walk out every noon for lunch, up North Broad Street; between the Temple and City Hall, he would give away every penny he had to the line of beggars and ne'er-do-wells lying in wait for him. But he always ate lunch. The laymen in his church had a standing agreement that some one of them was to be in City Hall Plaza, every day at noon, to meet the old saint and buy his lunch.

Once, in Rome, he became critically ill; a little Italian nurse in a Roman hospital saved his life. He put up a memorial stone to her in Baptist Temple, near the pulpit. Every time he entered the pulpit he would detour a little in order to brush the face of the stone bearing her name with the sleeve of his pulpit gown. . . .

Did you know that every penny he made on this lecture went to the founding of Temple University? When he died,

there was an insurance policy for Mrs. Conwell, but that
was about all. . . .

He has touched us all with **Acres of Diamonds.** He speaks
frequently in this lecture of his home city of Philadelphia.
But when he says "right here in Philadelphia" the reader
must understand that he means "right here in your home
town"-right here in Crosby's Corners, or Oshkosh, or
Midvale.

He found acres of diamonds in his own great soul; he can
show you diamonds, in yours. . . .

THE PUBLISHERS

When going down the Tigris and Euphrates rivers many years ago with a party of English travelers I found myself under the direction of an old Arab guide whom we hired up at Bagdad, and I have often thought how that guide resembled our barbers in certain mental characteristics. He thought that it was not only his duty to guide us down those rivers, and do what he was paid for doing, but also to entertain us with stories curious and weird, ancient and modern, strange and familiar. Many of them I have forgotten, and I am glad I have, but there is one I shall never forget.

The old guide was leading my camel by its halter along the banks of those ancient rivers, and he told me story after story until I grew weary of his story-telling and ceased to listen. I have never been irritated with that guide when he lost his temper as I ceased listening. But I remember that he took off his Turkish cap and swung it in a circle to get my attention. I could see it through the corner of my eye, but I determined not to look straight at him for fear he would tell another story. But although I am not a woman, I did finally look, and as soon as I did he went right into another story.

Said he, "I will tell you a story now which I reserve for my particular friends." When he emphasized the words "particular friends," I listened, and I have ever been glad I did. I really feel devoutly thankful that there are 1,674 young men who have been carried through college by this lecture who are also glad that I did listen. The old guide told me that there once lived not far from the River Indus an ancient Persian by the name of Ali Hafed. He said that Ali Hafed owned a very large farm, that he had orchards, grainfields, and gardens; that he had money at interest, and was a wealthy and contented man. He was contented because he was wealthy, and wealthy because he was contented. One day there visited the old Persian farmer one of those ancient Buddhist priests, one of the wise men of the East. He sat down by the fire and told the old farmer how this world of ours was made. He said that this world was once a mere bank of fog, and that the Almighty thrust His finger into this bank of fog, and began slowly to move His finger around, increasing the speed until at last He whirled this bank of fog into a solid universe, burning its way through other banks of fog, and condensed the moisture, until it fell in floods of rain upon its hot surface, and cooled the outward crust. Then the internal fires bursting outward through the crust threw up the mountains and hills, the valleys, the plains and prairies of this wonderful world of ours. If this internal molten mass came bursting out and cooled very quickly it became granite; less quickly copper, less quickly silver, less quickly gold, and, after gold, diamonds were made.

Said the old priest, "A diamond is a congealed drop of sunlight." Now that is literally scientifically true, that a diamond is an actual deposit of carbon from the sun. The old priest told Ali Hafed that if he had one diamond the size of his thumb he could purchase the county, and, if he had a mine of diamonds he could place his children upon thrones through the influence of their great wealth.

Ali Hafed heard all about diamonds, how much they were worth, and went to bed that night a poor man. He had not lost anything, but he was poor because he was discontented, and discontented because he feared he was poor. He said, "I want a mine of diamonds," and he lay awake all night.

Early in the morning he sought out the priest. I know by experience that a priest is very cross when awakened early in the morning, and when he shook that old priest out of his dreams, Ali Hafed said to him:

"Will you tell me where I can find diamonds?"

"Diamonds! What do you want with diamonds?" "Why, I wish to be immensely rich." "Well, then, go along and find them. That is all you have to do; go and find them, and then you have them" "But I don't know where to go." "Well, if you will find a river that runs through white sands, between high mountains, in those white sands you will always find diamonds." "I don't believe there is any such river." "Oh yes, there are plenty of them. All you have to do is to go and find them, and then you have them." Said Ali Hafed, "I will go."

So he sold his farm, collected his money, left his family in charge of a neighbor, and away he went in search of diamonds. He began his search, very properly to my mind, at the Mountains of the Moon. Afterward he came around into Palestine, then wandered on into Europe, and at last when his money was all spent and he was in rags, wretchedness, and poverty, he stood on the shore of the bay at Barcelona, in Spain, when a great tidal wave came rolling in between the pillars of Hercules, and the poor, afflicted, suffering, dying man could not resist the awful temptation to cast himself into that incoming tide, and he sank beneath its foaming crest, never to rise in this life again.

When that old guide had told me that awfully sad story he stopped the camel I was riding on and went back to fix the baggage that was coming off another camel, and I had an opportunity to muse over his story while he was gone. I remember saying to myself, "Why did he reserve that story for his 'particular friends'?" There seemed to be no beginning, no middle, no end, nothing to it. That was the first story I had ever heard told in my life, and would be the first one I ever read, in which the hero was killed in the first chapter. I had but one chapter of that story, and the hero was dead.

When the guide came back and took up the halter of my camel, he went right ahead with the story, into the second chapter, just as though there had been no break. The man who purchased Ali Hafed's farm one day led his camel into the garden to drink, and as that camel put its nose into the shallow water of that garden brook, Ali Hafed's successor noticed a curious flash of light from the white sands of the stream. He pulled out a black stone having an eye of light reflecting all the hues of the rainbow. He took the pebble

into the house and put it on the mantel which covers the
central fires, and forgot all about it.

A few days later this same old priest came in to visit Ali
Hafed's successor, and the moment he opened that
drawing-room door he saw that flash of light on the
mantel, and he rushed up to it, and shouted: "Here is a
diamond! Has Ali Hafed returned?" "Oh no, Ali Hafed has
not returned, and that is not a diamond. That is nothing but
a stone we found right out here in our own garden." "But,"
said the priest, "I tell you I know a diamond when I see it. I
know positively that is a diamond."

Then together they rushed out into that old garden and
stirred up the white sands with their fingers, and lo! there
came up other more beautiful and valuable gems than the
first. "Thus," said the guide to me, and, friends, it is
historically true, "was discovered the diamond mine of
Golcanda, the most magnificent diamond mine in all the
history of mankind, excelling the Kimberly itself. The
Kohinoor, and the Orloff of the crown jewels of England
and Russia, the largest on earth, came from that mine."

When that old Arab guide told me the second chapter of
his story, he then took off his Turkish cap and swung it
around in the air again to get my attention to the moral.
Those Arab guides have morals to their stories, although
they are not always moral. As he swung his hat, he said to
me. "Had Ali Hafed remained at home and dug in his own
cellar, or underneath his own wheat fields, or in his own
garden, instead of wretchedness, starvation, and death by
suicide in a strange land, he would have had 'acres of
diamonds.' For every acre of that old farm, yes, every
shovelful, afterward revealed gems which since have
decorated the crowns of monarchs."

When he had added the moral to his story I saw why he
reserved it for "his particular friends." But I did not tell
him I could see it. It was that mean old Arab's way of going
around a thing like a lawyer, to say indirectly what he did
not dare say directly, that "in his private opinion there

was a certain young man then traveling down the Tigris River that might better be at home in America." I did not tell him I could see that, but I told him his story reminded me of one, and I told it to him quickly, and I think I will tell it to you.

I told him of a man out in California in 1847, who owned a ranch. He heard they had discovered gold in southern California, and so with a passion for gold he sold his ranch to Colonel Sutter, and away he went, never to come back. Colonel Sutter put a mill upon a stream that ran through that ranch, and one day his little girl brought some wet sand from the raceway into their home and sifted it through her fingers before the fire, and in that falling sand a visitor saw the first shining scales of real gold that were ever discovered in California. The man who had owned that ranch wanted gold, and he could have secured it for the mere taking. Indeed, thirty-eight millions of dollars have been taken out of a very few acres since then. About eight years ago I delivered this lecture in a city that stands on that farm, and they told me that a one-third owner for years and years had been getting one hundred and twenty dollars in gold every fifteen minutes, sleeping or waking, without taxation. You and I would enjoy an income like that-if we didn't have to pay an income tax.

But a better illustration really than that occurred here in our own Pennsylvania. If there is anything I enjoy above another on the platform, it is to get one of these German audiences in Pennsylvania before me, and fire that at them, and I enjoy it tonight. There was a man living in Pennsylvania, not unlike some Pennsylvanians you have seen, who owned a farm, and he did with that farm just what I should do with a farm if I owned one in Pennsylvania-he sold it. But before he sold it he decided to secure employment collecting coal oil for his cousin, who was in the business in Canada, where they first discovered oil on this continent. They dipped it from the running

streams at that early time. So this Pennsylvania farmer
wrote to his cousin asking for employment. You see,
friends, this farmer was not altogether a foolish man. No,
he was not. He did not leave his farm until he had
something else to do. **Of all the simpletons the stars shine
on I don't know of a worse one than the man who leaves one
job before he has gotten another.** That has especial
reference to my profession, and has no reference whatever
to a man seeking a divorce. When he wrote to his cousin for
employment, his cousin replied, "I cannot engage you
because you know nothing about the oil business."

Well, then the old farmer said, "I will know," and with
most commendable zeal (characteristic of the students of
Temple University) he set himself at the study of the whole
subject. He began away back at the second day of God's
creation when this world was covered thick and deep with
that rich vegetation which since has turned to the
primitive beds of coal. He studied the subject until he
found that the drainings really of those rich beds of coal
furnished the coal oil that was worth pumping, and then he
found how it came up with the living springs. He studied
until he knew what it looked like, smelled like, tasted like,
and how to refine it. Now said he in his letter to his cousin,
"I understand the oil business." His cousin answered, "All
right, come on."

So he sold his farm, according to the county record, for
$833 (even money, "no cents"). He had scarcely gone from
that place before the man who purchased the spot went out
to arrange for the watering of the cattle. He found the
previous owner had gone out years before and put a plank
across the brook back of the barn, edgewise into the surface of the water just a few inches. The purpose of that
plank at that sharp angle across the brook was to throw
over to the other bank a dreadful-looking scum through
which the cattle would not put their noses. But with that
plank there to throw it all over to one side, the cattle would
drink below, and thus that man who had gone to Canada

had been himself damming back for twenty-three years a flood of coal oil which the state geologists of Pennsylvania declared to us ten years later was even then worth a hundred millions of dollars to our state, and four years ago our geologist declared the discovery to be worth to our state a thousand millions of dollars. The man who owned that territory on which the city of Titusville now stands, and those Pleasantville valleys, had studied the subject from the second day of God's creation clear down to the present time. He studied it until he knew all about it, and yet he is said to have sold the whole of it for $833, and again I say, "no sense."

But I need another illustration. I found it in Massachusetts, and I am sorry I did because that is the state I came from. This young man in Massachusetts furnishes just another phase of my thought. He went to Yale College and studied mines and mining, and became such an adept as a mining engineer that he was employed by the authorities of the university to train students who were behind their classes. During his senior year he earned $15 a week for doing that work. When he graduated they raised his pay from $15 to $45 a week, and offered him a professorship, and as soon as they did he went right home to his mother. **If they had raised that boy's pay from $15 to $15.60 he would have stayed and been proud of the place, but when they put it up to $45 at one leap, he said, "Mother, I won't work for $45 a week. The idea of a man with a brain like mine working for $45 a week!** Let's go out in California and stake out gold mines and silver mines,

Said his mother, "Now, Charlie, it is just as well to be happy, too." And they were both right about it. As he was an only son and she a widow, of course he had his way. They always do.

They sold out in Massachusetts, and instead of going to California they went to Wisconsin, where he went into the employ of the Superior Copper Mining Company at $15 a week again, but with the proviso in his contract that he

should have an interest in any mines he should discover for
the company. I don't believe he ever discovered a mine,
and if I am looking in the face of any stockholder of that
copper company, you wish he had discovered something or
other. I have friends who are not here because they could
not afford a ticket, who did have stock in that company at
the time this young man was employed there. This young
man went out there, and I have not heard a word from him.
I don't know what became of him, and I don't know
whether he found any mines or not, but I don't believe he
ever did.

But I do know the other end of the line. He had scarcely
gotten out of the old homestead before the succeeding
owner went out to dig potatoes. The potatoes were already
growing in the ground when he bought the farm, and as the
old farmer was bringing in a basket of potatoes it hugged
very tight between the ends of the stone fence. You know in
Massachusetts our farms are nearly all stone wall. There
you are obliged to be very economical of front gateways in
order to have some place to put the stone. When that
basket hugged so tight he set it down on the ground, and
then dragged on one side, and pulled on the other side, and
as he was dragging that basket through this farmer
noticed in the upper and outer corner of that stone wall,
right next the gate, a block of native silver eight inches
square. That professor of mines, mining, and mineralogy,
who knew so much about the subject that he would not
work for $45 a week, when he sold that homestead in
Massachusetts sat right on that silver to make the bargain.
He was born on that homestead, was brought up there, and
had gone back and forth rubbing the stone with his sleeve
until it reflected his countenance, and seemed to say,
"Here is a hundred thousand dollars right down here just
for the taking." But he would not take it. It was in a home
in Newburyport, Massachusetts, and there was no silver
there, all away off-well, I don't know where, and he did not,
but somewhere else, and he was a professor of mineralogy.

My friends, that mistake is very universally made, and why should we even smile at him. I often wonder what has become of him. I do not know at all, but I will tell you what I "guess" as a Yankee. I guess that he sits out there by his fireside tonight with his friends gathered around him, and he is saying to them something like this: "Do you know that man Conwell who lives in Philadelphia?" "Oh yes, I have heard of him." "Do you know that man Jones who lives in Philadelphia?" "Yes, I have heard of him, too."

Then he begins to laugh, and shakes his sides, and says to his friends, "Well, they have done just the same thing I did, precisely"-and that spoils the whole joke, for you and I have done the same thing he did, and while we sit here and laugh at him he has a better right to sit out there and laugh at us. I know I have made the same mistakes, but, of course, that does not make any difference, because we don't expect the same man to preach and practice, too.

As I come here tonight and look around this audience I am seeing again what through these fifty years I have continually seen—men that are making precisely that same mistake. I often wish I could see the younger people, and would that the Academy had been filled tonight with our high-school scholars and our gammar-school scholars, that I could have them to talk to. While I would have preferred such an audience as that, because they are most susceptible, as they have not grown up into their prejudices as we have, they have not gotten into any custom that they cannot break, they have not met with any failures as we have; and while I could perhaps do such an audience as that more good than I can do grown-up people, yet I will do the best I can with the material I have. I say to you that you have "acres of diamonds" in Philadelphia right where you now live. "Oh," but you will say, "you cannot know much about your city if you think there are any 'acres of diamonds' here."

I was greatly interested in that account in the newspaper of the young man who found that diamond in North

Carolina. It was one of the purest diamonds that has ever been discovered, and it has several predecessors near the same locality. I went to a distinguished professor in mineralogy and asked him where he thought those diamonds came from. The professor secured the map of the geologic formations of our continent, and traced it. He said it went either through the underlying carboniferous strata adapted for such production, westward through Ohio and the Mississippi, or in more probability came eastward through Virginia and up the shore of the Atlantic Ocean. It is a fact that the diamonds were there, for they have been discovered and sold; and that they were carried down there during the drift period, from some northern locality. Now who can say but some person going down with his drill in Philadelphia will find some trace of a diamond mine yet down here? Oh, friends! you cannot say that you are not over one of the greatest diamond mines in the world, for such a diamond as that only comes from the most profitable mines that are found on earth.

But it serves simply to illustrate my thought, which I emphasize by saying if you do not have the actual diamond mines literally you have all that they would be good for to you. Because now that the Queen of England has given the greatest compliment ever conferred upon American woman for her attire because she did not appear with any jewels at all at the late reception in England, it has almost done away with the use of diamonds anyhow. All you would care for would be the few you would wear if you wish to be modest, and the rest you would sell for money.

Now then, I say again that the opportunity to get rich, to attain unto great wealth, is here in Philadelphia now, within the reach of almost every man and woman who hears me speak tonight, and I mean just what I say. I have not came to this platform even under these circumstances to recite something to you. I have come to tell you what in God's sight I believe to be the truth, and if the years of life have been of any value to me in the attainment of common sense, I know I am right; that the men and women sitting here, who found it difficult perhaps to buy a ticket to this lecture or gathering tonight, have within their reach "acres of diamonds," opportunities to get largely wealthy. There never was a place on earth more adapted than the city of Philadelphia today, and never in the history of the world did a poor man without capital have such an opportunity to get rich quickly and honestly as he has now in our city. I say it is the truth, and I want you to accept it as such; for if you think I have come to simply recite something, then I would better not be here. I have no time to waste in any such talk, but to say the things I believe, and unless some of you get richer for what I am saying tonight my time is wasted.

I say that you ought to get rich, and it is your duty to get rich. How many of my pious brethren say to me, "Do you, a Christian minister, spend your time going up and down the country advising young people to get rich, to get money?" "Yes, of course I do." They say, "Isn't that awful! Why don't you preach the gospel instead of preaching about man's making money?" "Because to make money honestly is to preach the gospel." That is the reason. The men who get rich may be the most honest men you find in the community.

"Oh," but says some young man here tonight, "I have been told all my life that if a person has money he is very dishonest and dishonorable and mean and contemptible." My friend, that is the reason why you have none, because you have that idea of people. The foundation of your faith is altogether false, Let me say here clearly, and say it briefly, though subject to discussion which I have not time for here, ninety-eight out of one hundred of the rich men of America are honest. That is why they are rich. That is why they are trusted with money. That is why they carry on great enterprises and find plenty of people to work with them. It is because they are honest men.

Says another young man, "I hear sometimes of men that get millions of dollars dishonestly." Yes, of course you do, and so do I. But they are so rare a thing in fact that the newspapers talk about them all the time as a matter of news until you get the idea that all the other rich men got rich dishonestly.

My friend, you take and drive me—if you furnish the auto—out into the suburbs of Philadelphia, and introduce me to the people who own their homes around this great city, those beautiful homes with gardens and flowers, those magnificent homes so lovely in their art, and I will introduce you to the very best people in character as well as in enterprise in our city, and you know I will. A man is not really a true man until he owns his own home, and they that own their homes are made more honorable and honest and pure, and true and economical and careful, by owning the home.

For a man to have money, even in large sums, is not an inconsistent thing. We preach against covetousness, and you know we do, in the pulpit, and oftentimes preach a-gainst it so long and use the terms about "filthy lucre" so extremely that Christians get the idea that when we stand in the pulpit we believe it is wicked for any man to have money—until the collection basket goes around, and then we almost swear at the people because they don't give more money. Oh, the inconsistency of such doctrines as that!

Money is power, and you ought to be reasonably am-bitious to have it. You ought because you can do more good with it than you could without it. Money printed your Bible, money builds your churches, money sends your missionaries, and money pays your preachers, and you would not have many of them, either, if you did not pay them. I am always willing that my church should raise my salary, because the church that pays the largest salary always raises it the easiest. You never knew an exception to it in your life. The man who gets the largest salary can do the most good with the power that is furnished to him. Of course he can if his spirit be right to use it for what it is given to him.

I say, then, you ought to have money. If you can honestly attain unto riches in Philadelphia, it is your Christian and godly duty to do so. It is an awful mistake of these pious people to think you must be awfully poor in order to be pious.

Some men say, "Don't you sympathize with the poor people?" Of course I do, or else I would not have been lecturing these years. I won't give in but what I sympathize with the poor, but the number of poor who are to be sympathized with is very small. To sympathize with a man whom God has punished for his sins, thus to help him when God would still continue a just punishment, is to do wrong, no doubt about it, and we do that more than we help those who are deserving. While we should sympathize with God's poor—that is, those who cannot help themselves—let us remember there is not a poor person in the United States who was not made poor by his own shortcomings, or by the shortcomings of someone else. It is all wrong to be poor, anyhow. Let us give in to that argument and pass that to one side.

A gentleman gets up back there, and says, "Don't you think there are some things in this world that are better than money?" Of course I do, but I am talking about money now. Of course there are some things higher than money. Oh yes, I know by the grave that has left me standing alone that there are some things in this world that are higher and sweeter and purer than money. Well do I know there are some things higher and grander than gold. Love is the grandest thing on God's earth, but fortunate the lover who has plenty of money. Money is power, money is force, money will do good as well as harm. In the hands of good men and women it could accomplish, and it has accomplished, good.

I hate to leave that behind me. I heard a man get up in a prayer-meeting in our city and thank the Lord he was "one of God's poor." Well, I wonder what his wife thinks about that? She earns all the money that comes into that house, and he smokes a part of that on the veranda. I don't want to see any more of the Lord's poor of that kind, and I don't believe the Lord does. And yet there are some people who think in order to be pious you must be awfully poor and awfully dirty. That does not follow at all. While we sympathize with the poor, let us not teach a doctrine like that.

Yet the age is prejudiced against advising a Christian man (or, as a Jew would say, a godly man) from attaining unto wealth. The prejudice is so universal and the years are far enough back, I think, for me to safely mention that years ago up at Temple University there was a young man in our theological school who thought he was the only pious student in that department. He came into my office one evening and sat down by my desk, and said to me: "Mr. President, I think it is my duty sir, to come in and labor with you." "What has happened now?" Said he, "I heard you say at the Academy, at the Peirce School commencement, that you thought it was an honorable ambition for a young man to desire to have wealth, and that you thought it made him temperate, made him anxious to have a good name, and made him industrious. You spoke about man's ambition to have money helping to make him a good man. Sir, I have come to tell you the Holy Bible says that 'money is the root of all evil.' "

I told him I had never seen it in the Bible, and advised him to go out into the chapel and get the Bible, and show me the place. So out he went for the Bible, and soon he stalked into my office with the Bible open, with all the bigoted pride of the narrow sectarian, or of one who founds his Christianity on some misinterpretation of Scripture.

He flung the Bible down on my desk, and fairly squealed into my ear: 'There it is, Mr. President; you can read it for yourself." I said to him: "Well, young man, you will learn when you get a little older that you cannot trust another denomination to read the Bible for you. You belong to another denomination. You are taught in the theological school, however, that emphasis is exegesis. Now, will you take that Bible and read it yourself, and give the proper emphasis to it?"

He took the Bible, and proudly read," 'The love of money is the root of all evil.' "

Then he had it right, and when one does quote aright from that same old Book he quotes the absolute truth. I have lived through fifty years of the mightiest battle that old Book has ever fought, and I have lived to see its banners flying free; for never in the history of this world did the great minds of earth so universally agree that the Bible is true—all true— as they do at this very hour.

So I say that when he quoted right, of course he quoted the absolute truth. "The love of money is the root of all evil." He who tries to attain unto it too quickly, or dishonestly, will fall into many snares, no doubt about that. The love of money. What is that? It is making an idol of money, and idolatry pure and simple everywhere is condemned by the Holy Scriptures and by man's common sense. The man that worships the dollar instead of thinking of the purposes for which it ought to be used, the man who idolizes simply money, the miser that hordes his money in the cellar, or hides it in his stocking, or refuses to invest it where it will do the world good, that man who hugs the dollar until the eagle squeals has in him the root of all evil.

I think I will leave that behind me now and answer the question of nearly all of you who are asking, "Is there opportunity to get rich in Philadelphia?" Well, now, how simple a thing it is to see where it is, and the instant you see where it is it is yours. Some old gentleman gets up back there and says, "Mr. Conwell, have you lived in

Philadelphia for thirty-one years and don't know that the time has gone by when you can make anything in this city?" "No, I don't think it is." "Yes, it is; I have tried it." "What business are you in?" "I kept a store here for twenty years, and never made over a thousand dollars in the whole twenty years."

"Well, then, you can measure the good you have been to this city by what this city has paid you, because a man can judge very well what he is worth by what he receives; that is, in what he is to the world at this time. If you have not made over a thousand dollars in twenty years in Philadelphia, it would have been better for Philadelphia if they had kicked you out of the city nineteen years and nine months ago. A man has no right to keep a store in Philadelphia twenty years and not make at least five hundred thousand dollars in a store now." Oh, my friends, if you will just take only four blocks around you, and find out what the people want and what you ought to supply and set them down with your pencil, and figure up the profits you would make if you did supply them, you would very soon see it. There is wealth right within the sound of your voice.

Someone says: "You don't know anything about business. A preacher never knows a thing about business." Well, then, I will have to prove that I am an expert. I don't like to do this, but I have to do it because my testimony will not be taken if I am not an expert. My father kept a country store, and if there is any place under the stars where a man gets all sorts of experience in every kind of mercantile transactions, it is in the country store. I am not proud of my experience, but sometimes when my father was away he would leave me in charge of the store, though fortunately for him that was not very often. But this did occur many times, friends: A man would come in the store and say to me, "Do you keep jackknives?" "No, we don't keep jackknives," and I went off whistling a tune. What did I care about that man, anyhow? Then another farmer would come in and say, "Do you keep jackknives?" "No, we don't keep jackknives." Then I went away and whistled another tune. Then a third man came right in the same door and said, "Do you keep jackknives?" "No. Why is everyone around here asking for jackknives? Do you suppose we are keeping this store to supply the whole neighborhood with jackknives?" Do you carry on your store like that in Philadelphia? The difficulty was I had not then learned that the foundation of godliness and the foundation principle of success in business are both the same precisely. The man who says, "I cannot carry my religion into business" advertises himself either as being an imbecile in business, or on the road to bankruptcy, or a thief, one of the three, sure. He will fail within a very few years. He certainly will if he doens't carry his religion into business. If I had been carrying on my father's store on a Christian plan, godly plan, I would have had a jackknife for the third man when he called for it. Then I would have actually done him a kindness, and I would have received a reward myself, which it would have been my duty to take.

There are some overpious Christian people who think if you take any profit on anything you sell that you are an unrighteous man. On the contrary, you would be a criminal to sell goods for less than they cost. You have no right to do that. You cannot trust a man with your money who cannot take care of his own. You cannot trust a man in your family that is not true to his own wife. You cannot trust a man in the world that does not begin with his own heart, his own character, and his own life. It would have been my duty to have furnished a jackknife to the third man, or the second, and to have sold it to him and actually profited myself. I have no more right to sell goods without making a profit on them than I have to overcharge him dishonestly beyond what they are worth. But I should so sell each bill of goods that the person to whom I sell shall make as much as I made.

To live and let live is the principle of the gospel, and the principle of everyday common sense. Oh, young man, hear me; live as you go along. Do not wait until you have reached my years before you begin to enjoy anything of this life. If I had the millions back, or fifty cents of it, which I have tried to earn in these years, it would not do me anything like the good that it does me now in this almost sacred presence tonight. Oh, yes, I am paid over and over a hundredfold tonight for dividing as I have tried to do in some measure as I went along through the years. I ought not speak that way, it sounds egotistic, but I am old enough now to be excused for that. I should have helped my fellow men, which I have tried to do, and everyone should try to do, and get the happiness of it. The man who goes home with the sense that he has stolen a dollar that day, that he has robbed a man of what was his honest due, is not going to sweet rest. He arises tired in the morning, and goes with an unclean conscience to his work the next day. He is not a successful man at all, although he may have laid up millions. But the man who has gone through life dividing always with his fellow men, making and demanding his own rights and his own profits, and giving to every other man his rights and profits, lives every day, and not only that, but it is the royal road to great wealth. The history of the thousands of millionaires shows that to be the case.

The man over there who said he could not make anything in a store in Philadelphia has been carrying on his store on the wrong principle. Suppose I go into your store tomorrow morning and ask, "Do you know neighbor A, who lives one square away, at house No. 1240?" "Oh, yes, I have met him. He deals here at the corner store." "Where did he come from?" "I don't know." "How many does he have in his family?" "I don't know." "What ticket does he vote?" "I don't know." "What church does he go to?" "I don't know, and don't care. What are you asking all these questions for?"

If you had a store in Philadelphia would you answer me like that? If so, then you are conducting your business just as I carried on my father's business in Worthington, Massachusetts. You don't know where your neighbor came from when he moved to Philadelphia, and you don't care. If you had cared enough about him to take an interest in his affairs, to find out what he needed, you would have been rich. But you go through the world saying, "No opportunity to get rich," and there is the fault right at your own door.

But another young man gets up over there and says, "I cannot take up the mercantile business." (While I am talking of trade it applies to every occupation.) "Why can't you go into the mercantile business?" "Because I haven't any capital." Oh, the weak and dudish creature that can't see over its collar! It makes a person weak to see these little dudes standing around the corners and saying, "Oh, if I had plenty of capital, how rich I would get." "Young man, do you think you are going to get rich on capital?" "Certainly." Well, I say, "Certainly not." If your mother has plenty of money, and she will set you up in business, you will "set her up in business," supplying you with capital.

The moment a young man or woman gets more money than he or she has grown to by practical experience, that moment he has gotten a curse. It is no help to a young man or woman to inherit money. It is no help to your children to leave them money, but if you leave them education, if you leave them Christian and noble character, if you leave them a wide circle of friends, if you leave them an honorable name, it is far better then that they should have money. It would be worse for them, worse for the nation, that they should have any money at all. Oh, young man, if you have inherited money, don't regard it as a help. It will curse you through your years, and deprive you of the very best things of human life. There is no class of people to be pitied so much as the inexperienced sons and daughters of the rich of our generation. I pity the rich man's son. He can never know the best things in life.

One of the best things in our life is when a young man has earned his own living, and when he becomes engaged to some lovely young woman, and makes up his mind to have a home of his own. Then with that same love comes also that divine inspiration toward better things, and he begins to save his money. He begins to leave off his bad habits and put money in the bank. When he has a few hundred dollars he goes out in the suburbs to look for a home. He goes to the savings bank, perhaps, for half of the value, and then goes for his wife, and when he takes his bride over the threshold of that door for the first time he says in words of eloquence my voice can never touch: "I have earned this home myself. It is all mine, and I divide with thee." That is the grandest moment a human heart may ever know.

But a rich man's son can never know that. He takes his bride into a finer mansion, it may be, but he is obliged to go all the way through it and say to his wife, "My mother gave me that, my mother gave me that, and my mother gave me this," until his wife wishes she had married his mother. I pity the rich man's son.

The statistics of Massachusetts showed that not one rich man's son out of seventeen ever dies rich. I pity the rich man's sons unless they have the good sense of the elder Vanderbilt, which sometimes happens. He went to his father and said, "Did you earn all your money?" "I did, my son. I began to work on a ferryboat for twenty-five cents a day." "Then ," said his son, "I will have none of your money," and he, too, tried to get employment on a ferryboat that Saturday night. He could not get one there, but he did get a place for three dollars a week. Of course, if a rich man's son will do that, he will get the discipline of a poor boy that is worth more than a university education to any man. He would then be able to take care of the millions of his father. But as a rule the rich men will not let their sons do the very thing that made them great. As a rule, the rich man will not allow his son to work-and his mother!

Why, she would think it was a social disgrace if her poor, weak, little lily-fingered, sissy sort of boy had to earn his living with honest toil. I have no pity for such rich men's sons.

I remember one at Niagara Falls. I think I remember one a great deal nearer. I think there are gentlemen present who were at a great banquet, and I beg pardon of his friends. A a banquet here in Philadelphia there sat beside me a kindhearted young man, and he said, "Mr. Conwell, you have been sick for two or three years. When you go out, take my limousine, and it will take you up to your house on Broad Street." I thanked him very much, and perhaps I ought not to mention the incident in this way, but I follow the facts. I got onto the seat with the driver of that limousine, outside, and when we were going up I asked the driver, "How much did this limousine cost?" "Six thousand eight hundred, and he had to pay the duty on it." "Well," I said, "does the owner of this machine ever drive it himself?" At that the chauffeur laughed so heartily that he lost control of his machine. He was so surprised at that question that he ran up on the sidewalk, and around a corner lamp post out into the street again. And when he got out into the street he laughed till the whole machine trembled. He said: "He drive this machine! Oh, he would be lucky if he knew enough to get out when we get there."

I must tell you about a rich man's son at Niagara Falls. I came in from the lecture to the hotel, and as I approached the desk of the clerk there stood a millionaire's son from New York. He was an indescribable specimen of anthropologic impotency. He had a skullcap on one side of his head, with a gold tassel in the top of it, and a gold-headed cane under his arm with more in it than in his head. It is a difficult thing to describe that young man. He wore an eyeglass that he could not see through, patent-leather boots that he could not walk in, and pants that he could not sit down in-dressed like a grasshopper.

This human cricket came up to the clerk's desk just as I entered, adjusted his unseeing eyeglass, and spake in this wise to the clerk. You see, he thought it was "Hinglish, you know," to lisp. "Thir, will you have the kindneth to thupply me with thome papah and enwelophs!" The hotel clerk measured that man quick, and he pulled the envelopes and paper out of a drawer, threw them across the counter toward the young man, and then turned away to his books. You should have seen that young man when those envelopes came across that counter. He swelled up like a gobbler turkey, adjusted his unseeing eyeglass, and yelled: "Come right back here. Now thir, will you order a thervant to take that papah and enwelophs to yondah dethk." Oh, the poor, miserable contemptible American monkey! He could not carry paper and envelopes twenty feet. I suppose he could not get his arms down to do it. I have no pity for such travesties upon human nature. If you have not capital, young man, I am glad of it. What you need is common sense, not copper cents.

The best thing I can do is to illustrate by actual facts well-known to you all. A.T. Stewart, a poor boy in New York, had !1.50 to begin life on. He lost 87½ cents of that on the very first venture. How fortunate that young man who loses the first time he gambles. That boy said, "I will never gamble again in business," and he never did. How came he to lose 87½ cents? You probably all know the story how he lost itbecause he bought some needles, threads, and buttons to sell which people did not want, and had left them on his hands, a dead loss. Said the boy, "I will not lose any more money in that way." Then he went around first to the doors and asked the people what they did want. Then when he had found out what they wanted he invested hie 62½ cents to supply a known demand. Study it wherever you choose—in business, in your profession, in your housekeeping, whatever your life, that one thing is the secret of success. You must first know the demand. You must first know what people need, and then invest yourself where you are most needed. A.T. Stewart went on that principle until he was worth what amounted afterward to forty millions of dollars, owning the very store in which Mr. Wanamaker carried on his great work in New York. His fortune was made by losing something, which taught him the great lesson that he must only invest himself or his money in something that people need. When will you salesmen learn it? When will you manufacturers learn that you must know the changing needs of humanity if you would succeed in life? Apply yourselves, all you Christian people, as manufacturers or merchants or workmen to supply that human need. It is a great principle as broad as humanity and as deep as the Scripture itself.

The best illustration I ever heard was of John Jacob Astor. You know that he made the money of the Astor family when he lived in New York. He came across the sea in debt for his fare. But that poor boy with nothing in his pocket made the fortune of the Astor family in one principle. Some young man here tonight will say, "Well, they could make those fortunes over in New York, but they could not do it in Philadelphia!" My friends, did you ever read that wonderful book of Riss(his memory is sweet to us because of his recent death), wherein is given his statistical account of the records taken in 1889 of 107 millionaires of New York? If you read the account you will see that out of the 107 millionaires only seven made their money in New York. Out of the 107 millionaires worth ten million dollars in real estate then, 67 of them made their money in towns of less than 3,500 inhabitants. The richest man in this country today, if you read the real estate values, has never moved away from a town of 3,500 inhabitants. It makes not so much difference where you are as who you are. But if you cannot get rich in Philadelphia you certainly cannot do it in New York.

Now John Jacob Astor illustrated what can be done anywhere. He had a mortgage once on a millinery store,

and they could not sell bonnets enough to pay the interest
on his money. So he foreclosed that mortgage, took
possession of the store, and went into partnership with the
very same people, in the same store, with the same
capital. He did not give them a dollar of capital. They
had to sell goods to get any money. Then he left them alone
in the store just as they had been before, and he went out
and sat down on a bench in the park in the shade. What was
John Jacob Astor doing out there, and in partnership with
people who had failed on his own hands? He had the most
important and, to my mind, the most pleasant part of that
partnership on his hands. For as John Jacob Astor sat on
that bench he was watching the ladies as they went by: and
where is the man who would not get rich at that business?
As he sat on the bench if a lady passed him with her
shoulders back and head up, and looked straight to the
front, as if she did not care if all the world did gaze on her,
then he studied her bonnet, and by the time it was out of
sight he knew the shape of the frame, the color of the
trimmings, and the crinklings in the feather. I sometimes
try to describe a bonnet, but not always. I would not try to
describe a modern bonnet. Where is the man that could
describe one? This aggregation of all sorts of driftwood
stuck on the back of the head, or the side of the neck, like a
rooster with only one tail feather left. But in John Jacob
Astor's day there was some art about the millinery
business, and he went to the millinery store and said to
them: "Now put into the show window just such a bonnet
as I describe to you, because I have already seen a lady
who likes such a bonnet. Don't make up any more until I
come back." Then he went out and sat down again, and
another lady passed him of a different form, of different
complexion, with a different shape and color of bonnet.
"Now," said he, "put such a bonnet as that in the show
window." He did not fill his show window uptown with a lot
of hats and bonnets to drive people away, and then sit on

the back stairs and bawl because people went to Wan-namaker's to trade. He did not have a hat or a bonnet in that show window but what some lady liked before it was made up. The tide of custom began immediately to turn in, and that has been the foundation of the greatest store in New York in that line, and still exists as one of three stores. Its fortune was made by John Jacob Astor after they had failed in business, not by giving them any more money, but by finding out what the ladies liked for bonnets before they wasted any material in making them up. I tell you if a man could foresee the millinery business he could foresee anything under heaven!

Suppose I were to go through this audience tonight and ask you in this great manufacturing city if there are not opportunities to get rich in manufacturing "Oh yes," some young man says, "there are opportunities here still if you build with some trust and if you have two or three millions of dollars to begin with as capital." Young man, the history of the breaking up of the trusts by that attack upon "big business" is only illustrating what is now the opportunity of the smaller man. The time never came in the history of the world when you could get rich so quickly manufacturing without capital as you can now.

But you will say, "you cannot do anything of the kind. You cannot start without capital." Young man, let me illustrate for a moment. I must do it. It is my duty to every young man and woman, because we are all going into business very soon on the same plan. Young man, remember if you know what people need you have gotten more knowledge of a fortune than any amount of capital can give you.

There was a poor man out of work living in Hingham, Massachusetts. He lounged around the house until one day his wife told him to get out and work, and, as he lived in Massachusetts, he obeyed his wife. He went out and sat down on the shore of the bay, and whittled a soaked shingle into a wooden chain. His children that evening quarreled

over it, and he whittled a second one to keep peace. While
he was whittling the second one a neighbor came in and
said: "Why don't you whittle toys and sell them? You
could make money at that." "Oh," he said, "I would not
know what to make." "Why don't you ask your own
children right here in your own house what to make?"
"What is the use of trying that?" said the carpenter. "My
children are different from other people's children." (I
used to see people like that when I taught school. But he
acted upon the hint, and the next morning when Mary
came down the stairway, he asked, "What do you want for
a toy?" She began to tell him she would like a doll's bed, a
doll's washstand, a doll's carriage, a little doll's umbrella,
and went on with a list of things that would take him a
lifetime to supply. So, consulting his own children, in his
own house, he took the firewood, for he had no money to
buy lumber, and whittled those strong, unpainted
Hingham toys that were for so many years known all
over the world. That man began to make those toys for his
own children, and then made copies and sold them through
the boot-and-shoe store next door. He began to make a
little money, and then a little more, and Mr. Lawson, in his
FRENZIED FINANCE says that man is the richest man in
old Massachusetts, and I think it is the truth. And that man
is worth a hundred millions of dollars today, and has been
only thirty-four years making it on that one principle-that
one must judge that what his own children like at home
other people's children would like in their homes, too; to
judge the human heart by oneself, by one's wife or by one's
children is the royal road to success in manufacturing.
"Oh," but you say, "didn't he have any capital?" Yes, a
penknife, but I don't know that he had paid for that.

I spoke thus to an audience in New Britain, Con-
necticut, and a lady four seats back went home and tried
to take off her collar, and the collar button stuck in the
buttonhole. She threw it out and said, "I am going to get up

something better than that to put on collars." Her husband said; "After what Conwell said tonight, you see there is a need of an improved collar fastener that is easier to handle. There is a human need; there is a great fortune. Now, then, get up a collar button and get rich." He made fun of her, and consequently made fun of me, and that is one of the saddest things which comes over me like a deep cloud of midnight sometimes-although I have worked so hard for more than half a century, yet how little I have ever really done. Notwithstanding the greatness and the handsomeness of your compliment tonight, I do not believe there is one in ten of you that is going to make a million of dollars because you are here tonight; but it is not my fault, it is yours. I say that sincerely. What is the use of my talking if people never do what I advise them to do? When her husband ridiculed her, she made up her mind she would make a better collar button, and when a woman makes up her mind "she will," and does not say anything about it, she does it. It was that New England woman who invented the snap button which you can find anywhere now. It was first a collar button with a spring cap attached to the outer side. Any of you who wear modern waterproofs know the button that simply pushes together, and when you unbutton it you simply pull it apart. That is the button to which I refer, and which she invented. She afterward invented several other buttons, and then invested in more, and then was taken into partnership with great factories. Now that woman goes over the sea every summer in her private steamship-yes, and takes her husband with her! If her husband were to die, she would have money enough left now to buy a foreign duke or count or some such title as that at the latest quotations.

Now what is my lesson in that incident? It is this: I told her then, though I did not know her, what I now say to you, "Your wealth is too near to you. You are looking right over it"; and she had to look over it because it was right under her chin.

I have read in the newspaper that a woman never invented anything. Well, that newspaper ought to begin again. Of course, I do not refer to gossip-I refer to machines-and if I did I might better include the men. That newspaper could never appear if women had not invented something. Friends, think. Ye women, think! You say you cannot make a fortune because you are in some laundry, or running a sewing machine, it may be, or walking before some loom, and yet you can be a millionaire if you will but follow this almost infallible direction.

When you say a woman doesn't invent anything, I ask, Who invented the Jacquard loom that wove every stitch you wear? Mrs. Jacquard. The printer's roller, the print-ingpress, were invented by farmers' wives. Who invented the cotton gin of the South that enriched our country so amazingly? Mrs. General Greene invented the cotton gin and showed the idea to Mr. Whitney, and he, like a man, seized it. Who was it that invented the sewing machine? If I would go to school tomorrow and ask your children they would say, "Elias Howe."

He was in the Civil War with me, and often in my tent, and I often heard him say that he worked fourteen years to get up that sewing machine. But his wife made up her mind one day that they would starve to death if there wasn't something or other invented pretty soon, and so in two hours she invented the sewing machine. Of course he took out the patent in his name. Men always do that. Who was it that invented the mower and the reaper? According to Mr. McCormick's confidential communication, so recently published, it was a West Virginia woman, who, after his father and he had failed altogether in making a reaper and gave it up, took a lot of shears and nailed them together on the edge of a board, with one shaft of each pair loose, and then wired them so that when she pulled the wire one way it closed them, and when she pulled the wire the other way it opened them, and there she had the principle of the mowing machine. If you look at a mowing machine, you will see it is nothing but a lot of shears. If a woman can invent a mowing machine, if a woman can invent a Jacquard loom, if a woman can invent a cotton gin, if a woman can invent a trolley switch-as she did and made the trolleys possible; if a woman can invent, as Mr. Carnegie said, the great iron squeezers that laid the foundation of all the steel millions of the United States, "we men" can invent anything under the stars! I say that for the encouragement of the men.

Who are the great inventors of the world? Again this lesson comes before us. The great inventor sits next to you, or you are the person yourself. "OH," but you will say, "I have never invented anything in my life." Neither did the great inventors until they discovered one great secret. Do you think it is a man with a head like a bushel measure or a man like a stroke of lightning? It is neither. The really great man is a plain, straightforward, everyday, common-sense man. You would not dream that he was a great inventor if you did not see something he had actually done. His neighbors do not regard him as so great. You never see anything great over your back fence. You say there is no greatness among your neighbors. It is all away off somewhere else. Their greatness is ever so simple, so plain, so earnest, so practical, that the neighbors and friends never recognize it.

True greatness is often unrecognized. That is sure. You do not know anything about the greatest men and women. I went out to write the life of General Garfield, and a neighbor, knowing I was in a hurry, and as there was a great crowd around the front door, took me around to General Garfield's back door and shouted, "Jim! Jim!" And very soon "Jim" came to the door and let me in, and I wrote the biography of one of the grandest men of the nation, and yet he was just the same old "Jim" to his neighbor. If you know a great man in Philadelphia and you should meet him tomorrow, you would say, "How are you, Sam?" or "Good morning, Jim." Of course you would. That is just what you would do.

One of my soldiers in the Civil War had been sentenced
to death, and I went up to the White House in Washington
went there for the first time in my life-to see the President.
I went into the waiting room and sat down with a lot of
others on the benches, and the secretary asked one after
another to tell him what they wanted. After the secretary
had been through the line, he went in, and then came back
to the door and motioned for me. I went up to that an-
teroom, and the secretary said: "That is the President's
door right over there. Just rap on it and go right in." I
never was so taken aback, friends, in all my life, never.
The secretary himself made it worse for me, because he
had told me how to go in and then went out another door to
the left and shut that. There I was, in the hallway by
myself before the President of the United States of
America's door. I had been on fields of battle, where the
shells did sometimes shriek and the bullets did sometimes
hit me, but I always wanted to run. I have no sympathy
with the old man who says, "I would just as soon march up
to the cannon's mouth as eat my dinner." I have no faith in
a man who doesn't know enough to be afraid when he is
being shot at. I never was so afraid when the shells came
around us at Antietam as I was when I went into that room
that day; but I finally mustered the courage-I don't know
how I ever did-and at arm's length tapped on the door. The
man inside did not help me at all, but yelled out, "Come in
and sit down!"

Well, I went in and sat down n the edge of a chair, and
wished I were in Europe, and the man at the table did not
look up. He was one of the world's greatest men, and was
made great by one single rule. Oh, that all the young
people of Philadelphia were before me now and I could say
just this one thing, and that they would remember it. I
would give a lifetime for the effect it would have on our
city and on civilization. Abraham Lincoln's principle for
greatness can be adopted by nearly all. This was his rule:
whatsoever he had to do at all, he put his whole mind into it

and held it all there until that was all done. That makes
men great almost anywhere. He stuck to those papers at
that table and did not look up at me, and I sat there
trembling. Finally, when he had put the string around his
papers, he pushed them over to one side and looked over to
me, and a smile came over his worn face. He said: "I am a
very busy man and have only a few minutes to spare. Now
tell me in the fewest words what it is you want." I began to
tell him, and mentioned the case, and he said: "I have
heard all about it and you do not need to say any more. Mr.
Stanton was talking to me only a few days ago about that.
You can go to the hotel and rest assured that the President
never did sign an order to shoot a boy under twenty years
of age, and never will. You can say that to his mother
anyhow."

Then he said to me, "How is it going in the field?" I
said, "We sometimes get discouraged." And he said: "It is
all right. We are going to win out now. We are getting very
near the light. No man ought to wish to be President of the
United States, and I will be glad when I get through; then
Tad and I are going out to Springfield, Illinois. I have
bought a farm out there and I don't care if I again earn
only twenty-five cents a day. Tad has a mule team, and we
are going to plant onions.

Then he asked me, "Were you brought up on a farm?"
I said, "Yes; in the Berkshire Hills of Massachuetts." He
then threw his leg over the corner of the big chair and said,
"I have heard many a time, ever since I was young, that
up there in those hills you have to sharpen the noses of the
sheep in order to get down to the grass between the rocks."
He was so familiar, so everyday, so farmer-like, that I felt
right at home with him at once.

He then took hold of another roll of paper, and looked
up at me and said, "Good morning." I took the hint then
and got up and went out. After I had gotten out I could not
realize I had seen the President of the United States at all.
But a few days later, when still in the city, I saw a crowd

pass through the East Room by the coffin of Abraham
Lincoln, and when I looked at the upturned face of the
murdered President I felt then that the man I had seen
such a short time before, who, so simple a man, so plain a
man, was one of the greatest men that God ever raised up
to lead a nation on to ultimate liberty. Yet he was only
"Old Abe" to his neighbors. When they had the second
funeral, I was invited among others, and went out to see
that same coffin put back in the tomb at Springfield.
Around the tomb stood Lincoln's old neighbors, to whom he
was just "Old Abe." Of course that is all they would say.

Did you ever see a man who struts around altogether
too large to notice an ordinary working mechanic? Do you
think he is great? He is nothing but a puffed-up balloon,
held down by his big feet. There is no greatness there.
there.

Who are the great men and women? My attention was
called the other day to the history of a very little thing that
made the fortune of a very poor man. It was an awful
thing, and yet because of that experience he-not a great
inventor or genius-invented the pin that now is called the
safety pin, and out of that safety pin made a fortune of one
of the great aristocratic families of this nation.

A poor man in Massachusets who had worked in the
nail-works was injured at thirty-eight, and he could earn
but little money. He was employed in the office to rub out
the marks on the bills made by pencil memorandums, and
he used a rubber until his hand grew tired. He then tied a
piece of rubber on the end of a stick and worked it like a
plane. His little girl came and said, "Why, you have a
patent, haven't you?" The father said afterward, "My
daughter told me when I took that stick and put the rubber
on the end that there was a patent, and that was the first
thought of that." He went to Boston and applied for his
patent, and every one of you that has a rubber-tipped
pencil in your pocket is now paying tribut to the millionaire. No capital, not a penny did he invest in it. All was
income, all the way up into the millions.

But let me hasten to one other greater thought. "Show me the great men and women who live in Philadelphia." A gentleman over there will get up and say: "We don't have any great men in Philadelphia. They don't live here. They live away off in Rome or St. Petersburg or London or Manayunk, or anywhere else but here in our town." I have come now to the apex of my thought. I have come now to the heart of the whole matter and to the center of my struggle: Why isn't Philadelphia a greater city in its greater wealth? Why does New York excel Philadelphia? People say, "Because of her harbor." Why do many other cities of the United States get ahead of Philadelphia now? There is only one answer, and that is because our own people talk down their own city. If there ever was a community on earth that has to be forced ahead, it is the city of Philadelphia. If we are to have a boulevard, talk it down, if we are going to have better schools, talk them down; if you wish to have wise legislation, talk it down; talk all the proposed improvements down. That is the only great wrong that I can lay at the feet of the magnificent Philadelphia that has been so universally kind to me. I say it is time we turn around in our city and begin to talk up the things that are in our city, and begin to set them before the world as the people of Chicago, New York, St. Louis, and San Francisco do. Oh, if we only could get that spirit out among our people, that we can do things in Philadelphia and do them well!

Arise, ye millions of Philadelphians, trust in God and man, and believe in the great opportunities that are right here-not over in New York or Boston, but here-for - business, for everything that is worth living for on earth. There was never an opportunity greater. Let us talk up our own city.

But there are two other young men here tonight, and that is all I will venture to say, because it is too late. One over there gets up and says, "There is going to be a great man in Philadelphia, but never was one." "Oh, is that so?

When are you going to be great?'' ''When I am elected to some political office.'' Young man, won't you learn a lesson in the primer of politics that it is a **PRIMA FACIE** evidence of littleness to hold office under our form of government? Great men get into office sometimes, but what this country needs is men that will do what we tell them to do. This nation-where the people rule-is governed by the people, for the people, and so long as it is, then the officeholder is but the servant of the people, and the Bible says the servant cannot be greater than the master. The Bible says, ''He that is sent cannot be greater than He who sent him.'' The people rule, or should rule, and if they do, we do not need the greater men in office. If the great men in America took our offices, we would change to an empire in the next ten years.

I know of a great many young women, now that woman's suffrage is coming, who say, ''I am going to be President of the United States some day.'' I believe in woman's suffrage, and there is no doubt but what it is coming, and I am getting out of the way, anyhow. I may want an office by and by myself; but if the ambition for an office influences the women in their desire to vote, I want to say right here what I say to the young men, that if you only get the privilege of casting one vote, you don't get anything that is worth while. Unless you can control more than one vote, you will be unknown, and your influence so dissipated as practically not to be felt. This is governed by influence. It is governed by the ambitions and the enterprises which control votes. The young woman who thinks she is going to vote for the sake of holding an office is making an awful blunder.

That other young man gets up and says, ''There are going to be great men in this country and in Philadelphia.'' ''Is that so? When?'' ''When there comes a great war, when we get into difficuly through watchful waiting in Mexico; when we get into war with England over some frivolous deed, or with Japan or China or New Jersey or some distant country. Then I will march up to the cannon's mouth; I will sweep up among the glistening bayonets; I will leap into the arena and tear down the flag and bear it away in triumph. I will come home with stars on my shoulder, and hold every office in the gift of the nation, and I will be great.''No, you won't. You think you are going to be made great by an office, but remember that if you are not great before you get the office, you won't be great when you secure it. It will only be a burlesque in that shape.

We had a Peace Jubliee here after the Spanish War. Out west they don't believe this, because they said, "Philadelphia would not have heard of any Spanish War until fifty years hence." Some of you saw the procession go up Broad Street. I was away, but the family wrote to me that the tally-ho coach with Lieutenant Hobson upon it stopped right at the front door and the people shouted, "Hurrah for Hobson!' and if I had been there I would have yelled too, because he deserves much more of his country than he has ever received. But suppose I go into school and say, "Who sank the **MERRIMAC** at Santiago?" and if the boys answer me, "Hobson," they will tell me seveneighths of a lie. There were seven other heroes on that steamer, and they, by virtue of their position, were continually exposed to the Spanish fire, while Hobson, as an officer, might reasonably be behind the smokestack. You have gathered in this house your most intelligent people, and yet, perhaps, not one here can name the other seven men.

We ought not to so teach history. We ought to teach that, however humble a man' station may be, if he does his full duty in that place he is just as much entitled to the American people's honor as is the king upon his throne. But we do not so teach. We are now teaching everywhere that the generals do all the fighting.

I remember that, after the war, I went down to see General Robert E. Lee, that magnificent Christian gentleman of whom both North and South are now proud as

one of our great Americans. The general told me about his
Servant, Rastus, I hear that all the rest of your company
are killed, and why are you not killed?" Rastus winked at
him and said, "'Cause when there is any fightin' goin' on I
stay back with the generals."

I remember another illustration. I would leave it out
but for the fact that when you go to the library to read this
lecture, you will find this has been printed in it for twenty-
five years. I shut my eyes-shut them close-and lo! I see the
faces of my youth. Yes they sometimes say to me, "Your
hair is not white; you are working night and day without
seeming ever to stop; you can't be old." But when I shut
my eyes, like any other man of my years, oh, then come
trooping back the faces of the loved and lost of long ago,
and I know, whatever men may say, it is evening time.

I shut my eyes now and look back to my native town in
Massachusetts, and I see the cattle-show ground on the
mountaintop; I can see the horse sheds there. I can see the
Congregational Church; see the town hall and moun-
taineers' cottages; see a great assembly of people turning
out. dressed resplendently, and I can see flags flying and
handkerchiefs waving and hear bands playing. I can see
that company of soldiers that had re-enlised marching up
on that cattle-show ground. I was but a boy, but I was
captain of that company and puffed out with pride. A
cambric needle would have burst me all to pieces. Then I
thought it was the greatest event that ever came to man on
earth. If you have ever thought you would like to be a king
or queen, you go and be received by the mayor.

The bands played, and all the people turned out to
receive us. I marched up that Common so proud at the
head of my troops, and we turned down into the town hall.
Then they seated my soldiers down the center aisle and I
sat down on the front seat. A great assembly of people-a
hundred or two-came in to fill the town hall, so that they
stood up all around. Then the town officers came in and
formed a half circle. The mayor of the town sat in the

middle of the platform. He was a man who had never held office before; but he was a good man, and his friends have told me that I might use this without giving them offense. He was a good man, but he thought an office made a man great. He came up and took his seat, adjusted his powerful spectacles, and looked around, when he suddenly spied me sitting there on the front seat. He came right forward on the platform and invited me up to sit with the town officers. No town officer ever took any notice of me before I went to war, except to advise the teacher to thrash me, and now I was invited up on the stand with the town officers. Oh my! the town mayor was then the emperor, the king of our day and our time. As I came up on the platform they gave me a chair about this far, I would say, from the front.

When I had got seated, the chairman of the Selectmen arose and came forward to the table, and we all supposed he would introduce the Congregational minister, who was the only orator in town, and that he would give the oration to the returning soldiers. But, friends, you should have seen the surprise which ran over the audience when they discovered that the old fellow was going to deliver that speech himself. He had never made a speech in his life, but he fell into the same error that hundreds of other men have fallen into. It seems so strange that a man won't learn he must speak his piece as a boy if he intends to be an orator when he is grown, but he seems to think all he has to do is to hold as office to be a great orator.

So he came up to the front, and brought with him a speech which he had learned by heart walking up and down the pasture, where he had frightened the cattle. He brought the manuscript with him and spread it out on the table so as to be sure he might see it. He adjusted his spectacles and leaned over it for a moment and marched back on that platform, and then came forward like this-tramp, tramp, tramp. He must have studied the subject a great deal, when you come to think of it, because he assumed an "elocutionary" attitude. He rested heavily upon his left heel, threw back his shoulders, slightly advanced the right foot, opened the organs of speech, and advanced his right foot at an angle of forty-five. As he stood in that elocutionary attitude, friends, this is just the way that speech went. Some people say to me, "Don't you exagerate?" That would be impossible. But I am here for the lesson and not for the story, and this is the way it went:

"Fellow citizens-"- As soon as he heard his voice his fingers began to go like that, his knees began to shake, and then he trembled all over. He choked and swallowed and came around to the table to look at the manuscript. Then he gathered himself up with clenched fists and came back: "Fellow citizens, we are-Fellow citizens, we are-we are-we are- we are- we are- we are very happy-we are very happy - we are very happy. We are very happy to welcome back to their native town these soldiers who have fought and bled-and come back again to their native town. We are especially pleased to see with us today this young hero" (that meant me)-"this young hero in imagination" (friends, remember he said that; if he had not said "in imagination" I would not be egotistic enough to refer to it at all)-"this young hero who in imagination we have seen leading-we have seen leading-leading. We have seen leading his troops on to the deadly breach. We have seen his shining-we have seen his shining-his shining-his shining sword-flashing. Flashing in the sunlight, as he shouted to his troops, 'Come on'!"

Oh dear, dear, dear! how little that good man knew about war. If he had known anything about war at all he ought to have known what any of my G.A.R. comrades here tonight will tell you is true, that it is next to a crime for an officer of infantry ever in time of danger to go ahead of his men. "He, with his shining word flashing in the sunlight, shouting to his troops, 'Come on'!" I never did it. Do you suppose I would get in front of my men to be shot in front by the enemy and in the back by my own men? That is no place for an officer. The place for the officer in actual

battle is behind the line. How often, as a staff officer, I rode
down the line, when our men were suddenly called to the
line of battle, and the Rebel yells were coming out of the
woods, and shouted: "Officers to the rear! Officers to the
rear!" Then every officer gets behind the line of private
soldiers, and the higher the officer's rank the farther
behind he goes. Not because he is any the less brave, but
because the laws of war require that. And yet he shouted,
"He, with his sword-" In that house there sat the company of my soldiers who had carried that boy across the
Carolina rivers that he might not wet his feet. Some of
them had gone far out to get a pig or a chicken. Some of
them had gone to death under the shell-swept pines in the
mountains of Tennessee, yet in the good man's speech they
were scarcely known. He did refer to them, but only in-
cidentally. The hero of the hour was this boy. Did the
nation owe him anything? No, nothing then and nothing
now. Why was he the hero? Simply because that man fell
into that same human error-that this boy was great
because he was as officer and these were only private
soldiers.

Oh, I learned the lesson then that I will never forget so
long as the tongue of the bell of time continues to swing for
me. Greatness consists not in the holding of some future
office, but really consists in doing great deeds with little
means and the accomplishment of vast purpose from the
private ranks of life. To be great at all one must be great
here, now, in Philadelphia. He who can give to this city
better streets and better sidewalks, better schools and
more colleges, more happiness and more civilization,
more of God, he will be great anywhere. Let every man or
woman here, if you never hear my again, remember this,
that if you wish to be great at all, you must begin where
you are and with what you are, in Philadelphia, now. He
who can give to his city any blessing, he who can be a good
citizen while he lives here, he who can make better homes,

he who can be a blessing whether he works in the shop or
sits behind the counter or keeps house, whatever be his
life, he who would be great anywhere must first be great in
his own Philadelphia.

THE RICHEST MAN IN BABYLON

In Old Babylon here once lived a certain very rich man named Arkad. Far and wide he was famed for his liberality. He was generous in his charities. He was generous with his family. He was liberal in his own expenses. But nevertheless each year his wealth increased more rapidly than he spent it.

And there were certain friends of younger days who came to him and said: "You, Arkad, are more fortunate than we. You have become the richest man in all Babylon while we struggle for existence. You wear the finest garments and you enjoy the rarest foods, while we must be content to clothe our families in raiment that is presentable and feed them as best we may.

"Yet, once we were equal. We studied under the same master; we played in the same games. In neither the studies not the games did you outshine us. And in the years since, you have been no more an honorable citizen than we.

"Nor, have you worked harder or more faithfully, in so far as we can judge. Why then, should a fickle fate single you out to enjoy all the good things of life and ignore us who are equally deserving?"

Thereupon Arkad remonstrated with them, saying, "If you have not acquired more than a bare existence in the years since we were youths, it is because you either have failed to learn the laws that govern the building of wealth, or else you do not observe them.

" 'Fickle Fate' is a vicious goddess who brings no permanent good to anyone. On the contrary she brings ruin to almost every man upon whom she showers unearned gold. She makes wanton spenders, who soon dissipate all they receive and are left beset by overwhelming appetites and desires they have not the ability to gratify. Yet others whom she favors become misers and hoard their wealth, fearing to spend what they have not the ability to replace. They further are beset by fear of robbers and doom themselves to lives of emptiness and secret misery.

"Others, there probably are, who can take unearned gold and add to it and continue to be happy and contented citizens. But so few are they, I know of them but by hearsay. Think you of the men who have inherited sudden wealth, and see if these things are not so."

His friends admitted that of the men they knew who had inherited wealth, these words were true, and they besought him to explain to them how he had become possessed of so much property, so he continued:

"In my youth I looked about me and saw all the good things there were to bring happiness and contentment. And I realized that wealth increased the potency of all these.

"Wealth is a power. With wealth many things are possible.

"One may ornament the home with the richest of furnishings.

"One may sail the distant seas.

"One may feast on the delicacies of far lands.

"One may buy the ornaments of the gold worker and the stone polisher.

"One may even build mighty temples for the Gods.

"One may do all these things and many others in which there is delight for the senses and gratification for the soul.

"And when I realized all this I declared to myself that I would claim my share of the good things of life. I would not be one of those who stand afar off, enviously watching others enjoy. I would not be content to clothe myself in the cheapest raiment that looked respectable. I would not be satisified with the loss of a poor man. On the contrary, I would make myself a guest at this banquet of good things.

"Being, as you know, the son of a humble merchant, one of a large family with no hope of an inheritance, and not being endowed, as you have so frankly said, with superior powers or wisdom, I decided that if I was to achieve what I desired, time and study would be required.

"As for time, all men have it in abundance. You, each of you, have let slip by sufficient to have made yourselves wealthy. Yet you admit you have nothing to show except your good families of which you can be justly proud.

"As for study, did not our wise teacher teach us that learning was of two kinds; the one kind being the things we learned and knew, and the other being in the training that taught us how to find out what we did not know?

"Therefore, did I decide to find out how one might accumulate wealth, and when I had found out, to make this my task and do it well. For, is it not wise that we should enjoy while we dwell in the brightness of the sunshine, for sorrows enough shall descend upon us when we depart for the darkness of the world of spirit?

"I found employment as a scribe in the hall of records, and long hours each day I labored upon the clay tablets. Week after week, and month after month, I labored, yet for my earnings I had nought to show. Food and clothing and penance to the gods, and other things of which I could remember absorbed my earnings. But my determination did not leave me.

"One day Algamish, the money lender, came to the house of the city master and ordered a copy of the Ninth Law, and he said to me, 'I must have this in two days, and if the task is done by that time, two coppers will I give to thee.'

"So I labored hard, but the law was long, and when Algamish returned the task was unfinished. He was angry, and had I been his slave he would have beaten me. But knowing the city master would not permit him to injure me, I was unafraid, so I said to him.

" 'Algamish, you are a very rich man. Tell me how I may also become rich, and all night I will carve upon the clay, and when the sun rises it shall be completed.'

"He smiled at me and replied, 'You are a forward knave, but we will call it a bargain.'

"All that night I carved, though my back pained and the smell of the wick made my head ache until my eyes could hardly see. But when he returned at sunup the tablets were complete.

" 'Now,' I said, 'tell me what you promised.'

" 'You have fulfilled your part of our bargain, my son,' he said to me kindly, 'and I am ready to fulfill mine. I will tell you these things you wish to know because I am an old man, and an old tongue loves to wag. When youth comes to age for advice he receives the wisdom of years. But too often does youth think that age knows only the wisdom of days that are gone, and therefore profits not, but remember this, the sun that shines today is the sun that shone when thy father was born, and will still be shining when thy last grandchild shall pass into the darkness.

" 'The thoughts of youth,' he continued, 'are bright lights, like the meteors that oft make brilliant the sky, but the wisdom of age is like the fixed stars that shine so unchanged that the sailor may depend upon them to steer his course.

" 'Mark you well my words, for if you do not you will fail to grasp the truth that I will tell you, and you will think that your night's work has been in vain.'

"Then he looked at me shrewdly from under his shaggy brows and said in a low, forceful tone, 'I found the road to wealth when I decided that a part of all I earned was mine to keep. And so will you.'

"Then he continued to look at me with a glance that I could feel pierce me but said no more.

" 'Is that all?' I asked.

" 'That was sufficient to change the heart of a sheep herder into the heart of a money lender,' he replied.

" 'But all I earn is mine to keep, is it not?' I demanded.

" 'Far from it,' he replied. 'Do you not pay the sandalmaker? Do you not pay for the things you eat? Can you live in Babylon without spending? What have you to show for your earnings of the past month? What for the past year? Fool! You pay to everyone but yourself. Dullard, you labor for others. As well be a slave and work for what your master gives you to eat and wear. If you did keep for yourself one-tenth of all you earn, how much would you have in ten years?'

"My knowledge of the numbers did not forsake me and I answered, 'As much as I earn in one year.'

" 'You speak but half the truth,' he retorted. 'Every gold piece you save, is a slave to work for you. Every copper it earns is its child that also can earn for you. If you would become wealthy, then what you save must earn, and its children must earn, and its children's children must earn, to bring the abundance you crave.

" 'You think I cheat you for your long night's work,' he continued, 'but I am paying you a thousand times over if you have the intelligence to grasp the truth I offer you.

" 'A PART OF ALL YOU EARN IS YOURS TO KEEP. It should be not less than a tenth no matter how little you earn. It can be as much more as you can afford. Pay yourself first. Do not buy from the clothes-maker and the sandal-maker more than you can pay out of the rest and still have enough for food and charity and penance to the gods.

" 'Wealth, like a tree, grows from a tiny seed. The first copper you save is the seed from which your tree of wealth shall grow. The sooner you plant that seed the sooner shall the tree grow. And the morefaithfully you nourish and water that tree with savings, the sooner may you bask in contentment beneath its shade. So saying, he took his tablets and went away.

"I thought much about what he had said to me and it seemed reasonable. So I decided that I would try it. Each time I was paid I took one from each ten pieces of copper and hid it away. And strange as it may seem I was no shorter of funds than before; and managed to get along without it. But often I was tempted as my hoard began to grow, to spend it for some of the good things the merchants displayed, brought by camels and ships from the land of the Phoenicians. But I wisely refrained.

"A twelfth month after Algamish had gone he again returned and said to me, 'Son, have you paid to yourself not less than one-tenth of all you have earned for the past year?'

"I answered proudly, 'Yes, master, I have.'

" 'That is good,' he answered, beaming upon me, 'and what have you done with it?'

" 'I have given it to Asmur, the brickmaker, who told me he was traveling over the far seas and in Tyre he would buy for me the rare jewels of the Phoenccians. When he returns we shall sell these at high prices and divide the earnings.'

" 'Every fool must learn,' he growled, 'but why trust the knowledge of a brickmaker about jewels? Would you go to the breadmaker to inquire about the stars? No, by my tunic, you should go to the astrologer. Your savings are gone, youth, you have jerked your wealth tree up by the roots. But plant another. Try again and next time if you would have advice about jewels, go to the jewel merchant. If you would know the truth about sheep, go to the herds-man. Advice is one thing that is freely given away, but watch that you take only advice worth having. He who takes advice about his saving from one who is inex-perienced in such matters, shall pay with his savings for proving the falsity of their opinions.' Saying this, he went away.

"And it was as he said. For the Phoenicians are scoundrels and sold to Azmur worthless bits of glass for gems. But as Algamish had bid me, I again saved each tenth copper, for I now had formed the habit and it was no longer difficult.

"Again, twelve months later, Algamish came to the room of the scribes and addressed me. 'What progress have you made since last I saw you?'

" 'I have paid myself faithfully,' I replied, 'and my savings I have entrusted to Agger the shieldmaker, to buy bronze, and each fourth month he does pay me the rental.'

" 'That is good. And what do you do with the rental?'

" 'I do have a great feast with honey and fine wine and spiced cake. Also I have bought me a young ass upon which to ride.'

"To which Algamish laughed. 'You do eat the children of your savings. Then how do you expect them to work for you? And how can they have children that will also work for you? First get thee an army of golden slaves and then many a rich banquet may you enjoy without regret.' So saying he again went away.

"Now did I again see him for two years, when he once more returned and his face wall full of deep lines and his eyes drooped, for he was a very old man. And he said to me, 'Arkad, hast thou yet achieved the wealth thou dreamed of?'

"And I answered, 'Not yet all that I desire, but some I have and it earns more, and its earnings earn more.'

" 'And do you still take the advice of brickmakers?'

" 'About brickmaking they give good advice,' I retorted.

" 'Arkad,' he continued, 'you have learned your lessons well. You first learned to live upon less than you earned. Next you learned to seek advice from those who were competent through their experiences to give it. And, lastly, you have learned to make gold work for you.

" 'You have taught yourself how to acquire money, how to keep it, and how to use it. Therefore, you are competent for a responsible position. I am becoming an old man. My sons think only of spending and give no thought to earning. My interests are large, to much for me to look after. If you will go to Nippur and look after my lands there, I shall make you my partner and you shall share in my estate.'

"So I went to Nippur and took charge of his holdings. And because I was full of ambition and because I had mastered the three laws of successfully handling wealth, I was enabled to increase greatly the value of his properties. So I prospered much, and when the spirit of Algamish departed for the sphere of darkness, I did share in his estate as he had arranged under the law."

So spake Arkad, and when he had finished, one of his friends said, "You were indeed fortunate that Algamish made of you an heir."

"Fortunately only in that I had the desire to prosper before I first met him. For four years did I not prove my definiteness of purpose by keeping one-tenth of all I earned? Would you you call a fisherman lucky who for years so studied the habit of fish that with each changing wind he could cast his nets about them? Opportunity is a haughty goddess who wastes no time with those who are unprepared."

"You had strong will power to keep on after you lost your first year's savings. You are unusual in that way," spoke up another.

"Will power!" retorted Arkad, "What nonsense. Do you think will power gives a man the strength to lift a burden the camel cannot carry, or to draw a load the oxen cannot budge? Will power is but the unflinching purpose to carry a task you set for yourself to fulfillment. If I set for myself a task, be it ever so trifling, I shall see it through. How else shall I have confidence in myself to do important things?"

And then another friend spoke up and said, "If what you tell is true, and it does seem as you have said, reasonable, then being so simple, if all men did it, there would not be enough wealth to go around."

"Wealth grows wherever men exert energy," Arkad replied, "If a rich man builds him a new palace, is the gold he pays out gone? No, the brickmaker has part of it and the laborer has part of it, and the artist has part of it. And everyone who labors upon the house has part of it. Yet when the palace is completed, is it not worth all it cost? And is the ground upon which it stands not worth more because it is there? Wealth grows in magic ways. No man can prophesy the limit of it. Have not the Phoenicians built great cities on barren coasts with the wealth that comes from their ships of commerce on the seas?"

"What then do you advise us to do?" asked still another of his friends. "The years have passed and we are no longer young men and we have nothing put by."

"I advise that you follow the wisdom of Algamish and say, '**A PART OF ALL I EARN IS MINE TO KEEP.**' Say it in the morning when you first arise. Say it at noon. Say it at night. Say it each hour of every day. Say it to yourself until the words stand out like letters of fire across the sky.

"Impress yourself with the idea Fill yourself with the thought. Then take whatever portions seem wise. Let it be not less than one-tenth and lay it by. Arrange your other expenditures to do this. But lay by that portion first. Soon you will realize what a rich feeling it is to own a treasure upon which you alone have claim. As it grows it will stimulate you. A new joy of life will thrill you. Greater efforts will come to you to earn more. For of your increased earnings, will not the same percentage be also yours to keep?

"Then learn to make your treasure work for you. Make it your slave. Make its children and its children's children work for you.

"Insure an income for thy future. Look thou at the aged and forget not that in the days to come thou also will be numbered among them. Therefore invest thy treasure with greatest caution that it be not lost. Usurious rates of return are deceitful sirens that sing but to lure the unwary upon the rocks of loss and remorse.

"Provide also that thy family may not want should the Gods call thee to their realms. For such protection it is always possible to make provision with small payments at regular intervals. Therefore the provident man delays not in expectation of a large sum becoming available for such a wise purpose.

"Counsel with wise men. Seek the advice of men whose daily work is handling money. Let them save you from such an error as I myself made in entrusting my money to the judgment of Azmur, the brickmaker. A small return and a safe one is far more desirable than risk.

"Enjoy life while you are here. Do not over-strain or try to save too much. If one-tenth of all you earn is as much as you can comfortably keep, be content to keep this portion. Live otherwise according to your income and let not yourself get niggardly and afraid to spend. Life is good and life is rich with things worth while and things to enjoy."

His friends thanked him and went away. Some were silent because they had no imagination and could not understand. Some were sarcastic because they thought one so rich should divide with old friends not so fortunate. But some had in their eyes a new light. They realized that Algamish had come back each time to the room of the scribes because he was watching a man work his way out of darkness into light. When that man had found the light, a place awaited him. No one could fill that place until he was ready for such an opportunity.

These latter were the ones, who, in the following years frequently revisited Arkad, who received them gladly. He counseled with them and gave them freely of his wisdom as men of broad experience are always glad to do. And he assisted them in so investing their savings that it would bring in a good interest with safety and would neither be lost nor entangled in investments that paid no dividends.

THE TURNING POINT in these men's lives came upon that day when they realized the truth that had come from Algamish to Arkad and from Arkad to them.

SUMMARY OF FOUR CLASSICS

The Art of Achieving Success has been beautifully illustrated in the Four Success Classics. This first section of this writing is meant to be a quick summary of pertinent ideas covered in the four classics with a few added thoughts. Following the summary we will synthesize a success formula!

The Magic Story: This story illustrated that there is a plus-entity and a minus-entity in every human body that is born into the world. Whichever one of these is favored by the flesh becomes dominant; then the other is inclined to abandon its habitation, temporarily or for all time.

Everyone of us experience in our lives situations that depress us and drag us down. Our level of happiness and peace is but a graphic line that can be charted by its fluctuations upward and downward. Without a conserted effort we tend to have more downward swings and will dwell more at the bottom of the chart. Within each one's maturing process comes a time when we must cease concentrating on our failures, cease dwelling on the negative, cease feeling that we are nothing. We must cast off the minus-entity and refuse to allow its entry into our mind. We in turn fill our mind with the plus-entity, positive thoughts, aspirations, dreams, success and achievement. We become so involved and busy in positive pursuits that the minus-entity keeps finding itself crowded out. To the plus-entity of man, all things are possible!

The message of the Magic Story is so vitally crucial to success in any facet of life. We must cease dwelling on past failures or longings and concentrate with enthusiasm on the goals and aspirations we have placed in front of us. We must be motivated to concentrate on the objective at hand.

SALUTATION OF THE DAWN (From the Sanshrit)

Listen! to the salutation of the dawn! Look to this day for its life; the very life of life. In its brief course lies all the varieties and realities of your existence; the bliss of Growth; the glory of action; the splendor of beauty. For Yesterday is already a dream, and tomorrow is but a vision; but today well lived makes every yesterday a dream of happiness, and every tomorrow a vision of hope. Therefore, look ye well to this day. Such is the salutation of the dawn.

As a Man Thinketh: This classic protrays the essential concept of believing in yourself and believing that you can control your destiny! BELIEF!!

A summary of some of the thoughts in this writing were:

A man's mind is likened to a garden, which may be intelligently cultivated or allowed to run wild. But whether cultivated or neglected, it must and will, bring forth. Just as a gardener cultivates his plot keeping it free from weeds, so may we tend the garden of our mind, weeding out all the wrong, useless, and impure thoughts, and cultivate flowers and fruits of right, useful, and pure thoughts. By pursuing this process, we sooner or later discover that we are the master gardener of our soul, the director of our life. By right thoughts, we ascend to divine perfection. By wrong thoughts, we descend below the level of the beast. Godlike character is not a thing of favor or chance, but is the natural result of continued effort in right thinking, the effect of long cherished association with Godlike thoughts.

You can not travel within and stand still without

We cannot directly choose our circumstances, but we can choose our thoughts, and so indirectly, yet surely, shape our circumstances. All that we achieve and all that we fail to achieve is the direct result of our own thoughts. As we think, so we are; as we continue to think, so we remain.

....."The Vision you glorify in your mind, the Ideal that you enthrone in your heart--this you will build your life by, this you will become."

Acres of Diamonds: This writing presents the idea that the honest search for wealth is not evil within itself, but it is healthy and right! It produces industry, and a personal involvement in helping others. The author describes how the basic rules of Christianity are the same rules which produce success in business. We provide and care for the needs of those around us. For example, if people need pocketknifes, we provide a service by having them on hand. He suggests that it is only right to obtain an honest profit for our services and the amount that we make is often directly related to the amount of good we are doing for our community.

He admits that there are more important things than wealth and that they should be sought first, but that this need not preclude a man from also obtaining wealth. He argues that money is not the root of all evil, but the "love" of money is--placing it above the more important things such as family, religion, happiness and love of neighbor. He continues with the thought that wealth can mean power and influence for good in the hands of good men. Money can print Bibles, build churches and send out missionaries.

He further concludes that men have foolishly sold their properties and have gone in search of diamonds, gold, oil, and silver, only to be left without them and to have the new owners of their lands discover on those very lands the wealth they were seeking. We need not chase rainbows, but begin where we are to find success. All we need to do is look around and sense the needs of others and we can create, invent and provide services that will in turn help us to find our acres of Diamonds.

The message of this classic is vital to our achieving success in the areas of wealth, for too many have felt that it is evil to be rich or seek riches. However this writing clearly illustrates that the very act of creating our we lth can often be the evidence of the amount of good we are doing in helping others and that once we have obtained wealth we can use it again to accomplish even more good! Good is accomplished twice over by a good man.

The Richest Man in Babylon: This fourth story provides the lesson of organizing a plan to provide the capital we may need to accomplish our goals. It teaches the essential need to save at least one-tenth of all we earn and no less and then to utilize our savings intelligently and make them grow. These ideas are captured in the line:

A Part of all You Earn is Yours to Keep!

He further suggests three important lessons to learn:
1st: To learn to live upon less than you earn.
2nd: To seek advice from those who are competent.
3rd: To make our wealth work for us and make the children (or profits) of our investment also work for us, with a caution not to eat the children of our savings.

THE SUCCESS PERSONALITY

Dream, Belief, Decision, Plan Motivation, Persistence!!

The author has now summarized some of the basic messages from the classic stories, but more important than the specific messages are the ideas and philosophy that should have been captured during their reading. Hopefully some of the concepts have engrained themselves into your philosophy and hopefully you have begun to organize them into some kind of a formula that you can constantly keep before you and review! It may be that the one your author has organized will come close to your own. As your author sees it, the following items are basic to the art of achieving success in whatever area you may be seeking success: Dream, Belief, Decision, Plan, Motivation, and Persistence!

1. DREAM OR DESIRE: First of all you must have some kind of a dream, some small desire for something. You need to allow that desire to work within you until the desire begins to grow in its intensity.

2. BELIEF OR FAITH: Next it is essential that you have a belief in yourself and faith that you can obtain that which you desire. If you can't believe, then you need to dream some more. You need to meditate more on your goals until you can actually believe it is possible to obtain that which you desire.

Whatever the mind of man can conceive and believe it can achieve!

There is nothing which belief plus burning desire cannot make real!

There are no limitations to the mind except those we acknowledge!

3. DEFINITE DECISION OR COMMITMENT: Once you believe it is possible to obtain your desire, then comes the next important step of making a clear cut and definite decision to do something about obtaining it. You know that you are capable of doing a lot of things, but often fail to commit yourself to doing anything about them. The world is full of braggards who are forever claiming what they are capable of doing, but the world is short on those who quietly decide and do something. You decision doesn't need to be verbally broadcasted to others. It is best kept to yourself or to very special confidents that believe in you. It is most important that you are emotionally involved and deeply committed to your decision.

4. ORGANIZED PLAN OF ACTION: Physically write out on a piece of paper exactly what it is that you want and be specific about the details of what you want. Remembering that you don't get anything from nothing, write down also what you plan to give to obtain your desire. Be specific again and write out all the steps you plan to follow. Your plan may alter in some of the details as you learn more about what needs to be done to achieve your goal. If it is a college degree you want, write out classes you will need to take, and a specific time in which you hope to obtain it. If you are attempting to develop an attribute of character, list the specific areas you plan to work on and exercises you plan on doing to achieve that element of character. If it is a sum of money you want, write down the exact sum of money, and then the services you plan to render in obtaining it and the specific date you plan to achieve your goal. Write these out and carry them with you and review them frequently. You should review them at least every morning and evening until you have achieved them. If it is an involved goal, establish intermediate goals and dates for their obtainment. Your plan may be extended over many years, but for your best success you need to establish at least yearly and monthly goals and often weekly and daily goals. Along with your written plan you may find a progression chart helpful in achieving some goals.

5. **MOTIVATION & ENTHUSIASM:** Many dreams die on the vine at their initial inception simply because the motivation wears down. If you are to achieve you need to revive the initial motivation constantly. There must be a positive state of mind, belief in its obtainment must be fortified, enthusiasm and a success consciousness must be renewed often. There must be an emotional involvement and an all consuming obession to accomplish most significant goals.

To understand motivation you need to understand how your sub-conscious mind works. It works when emotions are mixed with the thoughts and when the thoughts are continually re-enforced or repeated to your mind.

....**Thoughts which are mixed with any of the feelings of emotions constitute a magnetic force which attracts other similar and related thoughts!**

Faith is a state of mind which may be induced, or created, by affirmation or repeated instructions to the sub-conscious mind. These are called affirmations, you keep affirming what you believe or what you want. This whole process of self-suggestion is also referred to as auto-suggestion. The human mind is constantly attracting vibrations which harmonize with that which is dominating the mind. Or another way of saying it is:

LIKE THOUGHTS GATHER LIKE THOUGHTS!

Have you ever noticed that when you become depressed, your mind quickly gathers other depressing thoughts, other failures, other times that you have been hurt and throws them into the already depressed mind?

Some people allow themselves to become deeply depressed for long hours, and even days. In fact some are always
under a semi-cloud of depression because they haven't
learned the simple truth of "auto-suggestion." If they
would cast off depressing thoughts and concentrate on
positive thoughts, they would soon find that the whole thing
can work to their benefit. Haven't you also had days in
which everything seemed to go right? As you are happier
towards others, they tend to respond in kind to you, and the
snowball goes on.

We have a Christian duty to our fellow men to try and
bring happiness into their lives and if we are going to s-
ucceed with this pleasant task, we must first begin with
ourselves and learn to control our thoughts by feeding our
minds positive thoughts and they will in turn gather more
of the same! The mind is a creature of habit, it thrives
upon the dominating thoughts we feed it. The subconscious
mind makes no distinction between constructive and
destructive thought, it works with the material that we
feed it. Therefore, if you would be motivated, you must
think of thoughts that are motivational in nature: positive,
happy, and emotionally involving.

If you would achieve, keep your mind creatively active
on achieving your goal. The author would suggest you
memorize and repeat often this magical little line: **Like
Thoughts Gather Like Thoughts!** Utilized positively, this
line will bring peace, happiness and success to any en-
deavor. Focus your mind with full concentration upon your
objective at hand and gather in all the positive thoughts
you can create until you are excited and feel the drive of
the all achieving power of **Motivation**. The riches and
blessings of the earth await those who are motivated.
Therefore, become **Motivated!**

6. DEDICATED PERSISTENCE AND COURAGE:
Then lastly, you must physically be moving toward your
goals. The state of mind usually provides the motivation

that produces action, but it is possible to get bogged down in organizing and day dreaming at a high pitch of motivation and not go anywhere in reality. You must have the physical ability to follow through. You must be able to meet obstacles and either go around them or use them as stepping stones. You must be able to meet temporary defeat with new plans and new approaches. You must realize that meaningful achievement usually require great courage, sacrifice, persistence and "stickability." You should realize also the truth of the following:

Every failure brings with it the seed of an equivalent success!

The stories are endless of millionaires who made their millions because they capitalized on what they learned in some of their earlier failures!

Setting Goals and Aspirations: Sit down and write out a list of all the things you desire to be, achieve, or to have. Organize them into categories of your choosing. The author will list his six generalized categories. It is given only as an idea. Make yours to fit your own life:

Aspirations of Author

1. Spiritual Success: To worship God and develop my spiritual mind through study of the scriptures and meditations.
2. Personal Success: To be at peace within myself, tranquil, happy and healthful.
3. Family Success: To be a successful provider and to love my wife and family.
4. Social Success: To have many friends, to love my neighbor and to enjoy relaxations.
5. Education Success: To obtain desired degrees and develop my mind to think aggressively in many spheres.

6. Financial Success: First, to provide well for my family, second, to develop sufficient assets to accomplish the good I desire, and last, to develop a large net worth.

After you develop your generalized categories, then list the specific things you hope to be, achieve or have. List the degrees and classes you want in college, the accomplishments you want to make in your business or specialty. List the places you want to go, list the kind of home you want and the price, the specific make of car, etc. List all of the luxuries you would like and your total net worth you hope to obtain. The second list should be specific and avoid generalities!

After you feel you have listed all the things you hope to do in life, order them according to their greatest importance to you and pick out just one or two to start working on immediately. Don't make the mistake of diving into all of them at once. Pick some that you can achieve quickly and experience some success . It might be well to make long-range goals and some that can be obtained in shorter periods of time. Apply the success formula to each goal.

The author would be pleased to learn of your successes and how some of these ideas may have helped you. Any new ideas that you develop would also be most welcome. Please write:

John D. Hawkes
4663 Rainbow Drive
Salt Lake City, Utah 84107

Success Formula

1. **Dream:** Desire, need or goal.
2. **Belief:** Faith or conviction in ability to obtain goal.
3. **Decision:** Definite commitment to obtain desire.
4. **Plan:** Organized plan of action to obtain desire.
5. **Motivation:** Enthusiasm, all consumming obession.
6. **Persistence:** Dedicated courage to follow through!